Sarah Pinder is a barrister at Goldsmith Chambers, where she practises in the fields of immigration law with some family law (children). She has been recommended since 2014 as a Leading Junior barrister in Band 4 in immigration by the Legal 500.

Prior to joining the Bar, Sarah practised in immigration and asylum law as a senior caseworker in a not-for-profit organisation in South London. This has given her the advantage of experience in preparing cases before they reach appeal stage, which she has pooled with her wealth of experience in court hearings as a barrister.

Whilst practicing in all fields of immigration law, Sarah has developed a particular interest and specialism in technical areas of the Immigration Rules, including cases within the Points-Based System such as Tier 1 (Entrepreneur) applications. Sarah is often considered by her instructing solicitors as the "go-to" person for such cases. She also has considerable experience and skill in delivering training seminars and webinars in these areas of the law.

# A Practical Guide to Immigration Law and Tier 1 Entrepreneur Applications

# A Practical Guide to Immigration Law and Tier 1 Entrepreneur Applications

Sarah Pinder,
Barrister at Law,
Goldsmith Chambers, London

Law Brief Publishing

Published 2018 by Law Brief Publishing, an imprint of Law Brief Publishing Ltd
30 The Parks
Minehead
Somerset
TA24 8BT

www.lawbriefpublishing.com

Paperback: 978-1-911035-84-8

# PREFACE

Ever since its inception in 2008, the Tier 1 Entrepreneur route of the Points Based System has not only attracted much interest but it has also caused many a headache. That may also be true of other avenues in immigration law, particularly since 2012 when the Immigration Rules were overhauled and have since been described as *"something of a disgrace"*, *"so tangled that even (a) spider has difficulty controlling (them)"* and *"achiev(ing) a degree of complexity, which even the Byzantine Emperors would have envied"*!

Arguably though the Tier 1 Entrepreneur route does encapsulate these difficulties the most with incredibly complicated provisions and very proscribed specified evidence. It has not helped either that the requirements have been changed along the way and so initial applicants have had to adapt to rule changes half way through their journey to settlement. Nonetheless, applicants remain hopeful to overcome these complexities since the route does present an exciting and creative path towards residing in the UK and eventually permanent residence.

Through this guide, practitioners and applicants alike will receive an introduction to the Tier 1 Entrepreneur route and will be presented with a summary of all of the provisions within the Immigration Rules that they need to be aware in order to successfully prepare an application, whether this be the initial application for initial leave, an extension or indeed an application for indefinite leave to remain. I have tried to keep the guide as simple as possible and I have included practical tips wherever possible. The guide also includes the necessary references to case-law and other useful materials, such as the Home Office guidance published in this category.

The law and guidance covered in this guide is correct and up to date as of 16th July 2018. When preparing an application, it is crucial however to always check the Immigration Rules themselves in addition to using this guide or any other text so as to ensure that the most up-to-date version of the rules is being referred to.

I would also like to thank the following persons in enabling me to put this guide together: first, my family who supported me setting time aside to write the guide at the same time as going through chicken pox and a house move! My former colleagues at the Migrant Legal Action based in Camberwell, London where I used to work before coming to the Bar and in particular, Himat Lakhani who is the one who trained me in immigration law when I was a case-worker there. Last but not least, my colleagues at Goldsmith Chambers, who are the most caring and dedicated team of immigration lawyers and with whom I am privileged to work.

Sarah Pinder
July 2018

# CONTENTS

# CONTENTS

# CHAPTER ONE
# WHY APPLY FOR TIER 1 (ENTREPRENEUR) LEAVE AND WHAT DOES THIS ROUTE OFFER?

In this chapter, we will look at what the Tier 1 Entrepreneur route entails and what its main benefits are.

The Tier 1 Entrepreneur route has been part of the Points-Based System of the Immigration Rules since 2008. It effectively replaced the 'businessperson' and 'innovator' categories, which existed prior to that. On 6th April 2012, the Tier 1 (Post-Study Work) category was also closed and to replace it, the Tier 1 (Entrepreneur Graduate) category was created. We will not cover this category in detail within this guide, but we will see in the second and third chapters of this guide how this category may often be used to 'feed in' to a Tier 1 Entrepreneur application.

The Immigration Rules providing for this route can be found in Part 6A and specifically in paragraphs 245DB-245F. These are to be read in conjunction with paragraphs 35-52 of Appendix A of the Immigration Rules. An applicant needs to score 75 points under the 'attributes' criteria contained in Appendix A as well as 10 points for English language and 10 points for maintenance funds, reaching a total of 95 points.

The Home Office currently operates two forms of guidance for Tier 1 Entrepreneur applications. These are as follows and are available from the government's website:

- *Tier 1 (Entrepreneur) of the Points Based System – Policy Guidance*, version 07/2018 for applications made on or after 6th July 2018

- *Tier 1 (Entrepreneur)* - Version 21.0, published on 16th January 2018[1]

If you need to consult the Home Office guidance, it is best to check both publications as some matters are dealt in one but not the other. On the whole however, I have found the second piece of guidance more helpful as the first one tends to paraphrase the requirements that are already set out in the Immigration Rules while the second one tends to share a bit more of the case-worker's decision-making process. Older versions of each piece of guidance can also be accessed from the government's archive website and it is important to ensure that the right piece of guidance is consulted and relied upon depending on the timing of the application and ensuing decision.

If you or your client wants to set up a new business or run an existing business in the UK, being a Tier 1 Entrepreneur may be the route for you. The route is designed to encourage investment in the UK economy and to attract dynamic and skilled entrepreneurs to this country. A minimum of £50,000 is required for the purposes of investment. However, since the category's inception, further restrictions have been placed limiting the source of funding for those who seek to rely on making £50,000 available for investment. We will see in the third chapter of the guide that applicants will not face such restriction if they have access to

---

1 Note that this piece of guidance does not appear to have been updated, as at the time of publishing, from the changes in the Immigration Rules brought about on 6th July 2018. It is best however to check the government's website directly when needing to consult the guidance.

£200,000 for the purposes of investments as part of their business activity.

As part of this route, those who qualify for initial leave to enter or remain will be allowed to reside in the UK for a period of up to three years and four months, if granted entry clearance, and three years if granted when already in the UK. During this time, such persons will be expected to set up, take over or join the running of one or more businesses and to work for their business, including as a self-employed person, as a director or as a partner. They may also apply for their family members to accompany or join them in the UK. The conditions on their stay once granted will forbid applicants from working outside of their business, for example by being employed somewhere else and from having recourse to public funds[2].

After three years, a person may extend their leave to a further two years after which they will be entitled to apply for indefinite leave to remain provided they can demonstrate that they satisfy the relevant criteria, which will be looked at in detail in the third chapter of this guide. There is also the option of applying for permanent residence under what is known as the 'accelerated route' after having held the status of Tier 1 Entrepreneur for only three years, again if certain and fairly onerous criteria are met, which will also be looked at in the third chapter of this guide.

The main advantage of this route is that the substance of the applicant's business is entirely at their discretion, save for a restriction concerning residential and property development and management, which is considered in more detail in the second

2 For a definition of 'public funds', see paragraph 6 of the Immigration Rules and for further clarification as to what is meant by 'having recourse to public funds', see also paragraphs 6A-6C.

chapter. Otherwise, there may be restrictions placed upon them depending on the source of their funding but aside from this, an applicant would be free to set up or run a business in, more or less, whatever sector they wish. A large part of their application to the Home Office will initially rest on their business plan but as long as the applicant can justify their plans and projections, they have a wide choice of business sector.

Similarly, if the applicant's initial business venture fails or does not prove profitable, they should have time within the initial three years of their leave to formulate alternative business plans and to try and start again. The Home Office does not require an applicant to stick to their original business plan throughout their residence in the UK. With this in mind, an applicant will need to meet the requirements of the 'genuineness' test, which are covered in the fourth chapter of this guide, and evidence the various investments made into the relevant business. Thus, it is important to retain records and to try and document an applicant's journey as an entrepreneur as fully as possible.

The second advantage is that you can apply as a part of a team of two. This means that two applicants can team up and set up a new business or take over or join an existing business together as business partners. The main benefit is that the team members do not each have to possess the full amount of funding but instead, they are able to pool their respective funds together for these to add up to the required amount. They do not even have to each invest an equal amount of money as long as they have and have had an equal level of control over the funds earmarked for the business and on-ward investment, which we will look at in further detail in section b) of the third chapter in this guide.

The third and important advantage is that the funds, which are needed to qualify as a Tier 1 Entrepreneur and which will need to be invested in the business do not necessarily need to be the applicant's own funds. The entirety of the funds or part of these funds can be provided by what is known as a 'third party funder'. This may be a person known to the applicant, such as a family member or benefactor but also a person unrelated to the applicant who may have an interest in seeing the applicant's business venture started. Such third-party funding may also come from a UK or devolved government department, venture capital firm funding or UK seed competition funding. There are detailed evidential requirements to accompany any application based on third-party funding, also looked at in the third chapter of this guide, but this, in principle, does make the Tier Entrepreneur application route more accessible.

Having set out the main advantages and benefits of this points-based system (PBS) route, practitioners and those who wish to make an application need to be aware that the Immigration Rules providing for this route have been drafted in a very protracted and proscribed manner.

The complexities of the PBS have already been recognised by certain Court of Appeal judges when handing down judgments in several cases. In addition, on 17th April 2018, Lord Justice Irwin observed that "*the Immigration Rules are, in truth, something of a disgrace*". His comments were given in the context of the Peter Taylor Memorial Lecture for the Professional Negligence Bar Association[3].

---

3 https://www.judiciary.gov.uk/wp-content/uploads/2018/04/speech-lj-irwin-pnba-complexity-and-obscurity-16042018.pdf p.14

Earlier in 2018, as part of the judgment in *Mudiyanselage v Secretary of State for the Home Department* [2018] 4 WLR 5, [2018] EWCA Civ 65, Lord Justice Underhill also stated that *"the web of Rules and Guidance has become so tangled that even the spider has difficulty controlling it"*[4]. Underhill LJ had also stated in an earlier case – *Singh v Secretary of State for the Home Department* [2015] All ER (D) 146 (Feb), [2015] EWCA Civ 74 – that *"the aim should be that the Rules should be readily understandable by ordinary lawyers and advisers. That is not the case at present"*[5].

The Home Office also announced in October 2017 that the Law Commission had been requested to review the Immigration Rules and advise on how best to simplify these. The Commission has outlined the following:

> *"They (the Immigration Rules) are widely criticised for being long, complex, and difficult to use. They total 1033 pages in length. Statements of changes to the Rules are now frequent and detailed. Between 2012 and 2016, for example, and driven mainly by the introduction of a "points based" immigration system, the Rules increased in length by about 25%. It has also been suggested that the Rules are poorly drafted."*[6]

4 §14

5 §59

6 Thirteenth Programme of Law Reform - Law Com No 377 – 8th November 2017 - https://s3-eu-west-2.amazonaws.com/lawcom-prod-storage-11jsxou24uy7q/uploads/2017/12/13th-Programme-of-Law-Reform.pdf §2.35

Those seeking to apply under the Tier 1 (Entrepreneur) route and those advising in this area should therefore take great care to understand the relevant Immigration Rules and the evidence that is required in support of applications. This category of the Immigration Rules is no exception to the cases under the PBS, which were under consideration in the judgments cited from above. The onus is generally on applicants to demonstrate their meeting the relevant criteria and the Home Office does not generally adopt a flexible or sympathetic approach and will readily refuse applications on mere technicalities, with very often drastic consequences for the applicant.

# CHAPTER TWO
# COMMON CRITERIA AND KEY CONCEPTS FOR ANY TIER 1 ENTREPRENEUR APPLICATION

## GENERAL GROUNDS OF REFUSAL

All applicants, whether by way of entry clearance or in-country, must not fall foul of the refusal grounds set out in Part 9 of the Immigration Rules. In addition, when applying in-country, an applicant must not be in the UK in breach of immigration laws. There is one exception to this – if the applicant meets the requirements of paragraph 39E of the Immigration Rules. In brief, this stipulates that a period of overstaying amounting to 14 days prior to an application being submitted may be disregarded.

Another aspect of the Immigration Rules, which relates to an applicant's character is the general requirement, when applying for entry clearance, to provide a copy of a criminal record certificate from the relevant authority in any country in which they have been present for 12 months or more (whether continuously or in total) in the past 10 years, while aged 18 years old or over – paragraph 245DB(r)-(s). It is possible for applicants to provide an explanation (satisfactory to the decision-maker) for any failure to provide such a certificate.

## COMMON CRITERIA FOR ANY APPLICATION

Firstly, an applicant must be aged 16 years old or over. If an applicant is under 18 years old, they must have the support of their parents, legal guardian or their parent with sole legal responsibility as well as their consent to the arrangements for the applicant's travel to the UK and their reception and care in the UK.

Secondly, most applicants will need to satisfy the Home Office of the English language requirement. They can do this by either passing an approved English language test[1] with at least CEFR level B1 in reading, writing, speaking and listening or by having an academic qualification that was taught in English and is recognised by UK NARIC as being equivalent to a UK bachelors degree, masters degree or PhD. An applicant may be exempt from this requirement if they are a citizen of an English-speaking country. Before counting on this exception however, the Immigration Rules should be consulted in order to check if the applicant's country is listed.

Lastly, an applicant must be able to support themselves during their time in the UK. This requirement is common to all PBS applications and is covered by Appendix C of the Immigration Rules. The level of 'maintenance funds' required varies depending on whether the applicant is applying for entry clearance (£3,310) or for leave to remain (£945). The funds need to have been held by the applicant in a financial institution in the form of cash funds

1 The list of approved test centres can be found on the government's website - https://assets.publishing.service.gov.uk/government/uploads/system/uploads/attachment_data/file/698174/2018-04-06_-_Approved_Secure_English_Language_Tests_and_Test_Centres_.pdf - and is up to date as of 6th April 2018

under their own control on the date of the application and for a consecutive period of 90 days prior to this.

There are several other evidential requirements set out in Appendix C concerning bank statement formats and other such formalities, which practitioners and those wishing to apply in this category are advised to consult in advance of advising or submitting an application. There are also separate 'maintenance funds' levels and requirements for family members of a Tier Entrepreneur applicant.

## KEY CONCEPTS

There are key definitions, which practitioners need to be aware of and which will be at the forefront of any Tier 1 Entrepreneur application. These mainly relate to the concepts of 'business', 'spending' or 'investing' funds but also to concepts, which may well be regarded as fairly straight forward, such as 'money' and having money 'available'!

Taking each of these concepts in turn:

Business

The definition of 'business' for the purposes of the Immigration Rules is contained in Paragraph 245D(b):

> *"an enterprise as a sole trader, a partnership or a company registered in the UK"*

There are further definitions in Appendix A, notably that it will only be 'UK business(es)', which count as a 'business' for the purpose of being awarded points as a Tier 1 Entrepreneur – Paragraph 39(b) of Appendix A.

In Paragraph 39(c), the term 'UK business' is clarified but note that this is defined against the applicant providing 'specified evidence' of the following:

> *"A business will be considered to be a UK business if the applicant provides the specified evidence in this Appendix to show that:*
>
> *(i) it is trading within the UK economy,*
>
> *(ii) it has its registered office in the UK, or, in the case of multinational companies with no UK registered office, its head office in the UK, except where the applicant is registered with HM Revenue & Customs as self-employed and does not have a business office,*
>
> *(iii) it has a UK bank account, and*
>
> *(iv) it is subject to UK taxation."*

There is also a further definition concerning 'new businesses' – Paragraph 46 of Appendix A. A Tier 1 Entrepreneur during the currency of the leave can qualify if they set up one or more new businesses. For a new business to be classed as such, the business needs to be one which is set up by the applicant no earlier than 12 months prior to the date of the application, which led to the first grant of leave as a Tier 1 (Entrepreneur). This period is extended to 24 months if the applicant's previous form of leave was as a Tier 1 Graduate Entrepreneur. There is however no obligation for a Tier 1 Entrepreneur to have already set up a business prior to their application for leave. This can be done once the leave is granted. Many applicants would, in any event, find it difficult, if not impossible, to take steps towards setting up a business since they may still be abroad and not yet resident or may be residing in the UK in a capacity, which forbids them from working in a self-employed capacity.

Money and when this is 'available'

Without needing to labour the point, 'money' is defined in paragraph 40(a) of Appendix A as meaning *"cash, not Individual Savings Accounts or other assets such as stocks and shares"*. I find that the locker-room scene from the film Jerry Maguire with Cuba Gooding Jr repeatedly shouting *"Show me the money!"* is most effective as a reminder. The need for cash funds is also in stark contrast with the Tier 1 investor category, where the specified funds are not necessarily required as cash.

Pursuant to paragraph 245D(c)(i) of the Immigration Rules, having funds 'available' means that the monies are:

- In the applicant's own possession, or
- In the financial accounts of a UK business, on which they are relying to claim points, or
- Available from a third party or third parties named in the application under the terms of the declaration(s) referred to in paragraph 41(a)(vi) of Appendix A.

There are also some further definitions of the term 'available' to be aware of:

- Paragraph 39(a)(i) of Appendix A states that money is not available for Appendix A purposes if it also used or earmarked for the purpose of maintenance funds.

- An applicant cannot score points in Appendix A if money is available from a third party, where that third party is also another Tier 1 Entrepreneur migrant or is the business of another Tier 1 Entrepreneur migrant or a close family member of another Tier 1 Entrepreneur migrant – paragraph 39(a)(ii).

The first bullet point immediately above will in general be easy enough to avoid. It is what is set out in the second bullet point, which is trickier. It is thought that the rationale behind this insertion into the Immigration Rules is to avoid funds being 'recycled' and the Home Office losing track as to the original source of an applicant's funds. For example, if a Tier 1 migrant has obtained leave on the basis of possessing £200,000 in cash but then acts as a third party funder in someone else's application, it may be difficult for the Home Office to satisfy themselves that the same funds are not being used for both applications.

Of course, applicants in most cases would have been able to submit evidence to demonstrate the contrary to the Home Office but it appears that the government wished to draw a bright line and avoid any difficulties arising from any such scenarios. This does place an onus on applicants and those advising them to conduct much more detailed enquiries before proceeding with an application. Not only will a third party's documentation and funds need to be checked but also instructions will need to be taken as to the third party's immigration status and whether they have a close family member who is a Tier 1 Entrepreneur migrant already.

The added difficulty is that the Home Office does not seek to define what is meant by 'close family member'. The Home Office guidance does not elaborate on this either. You would certainly be advised to apply common sense and treat anybody from the third party funder's immediate family as a 'close family member'. Anybody beyond these immediate family ties would still need to be looked at closely and applicants may prefer to avoid any family links where there are Tier 1 Entrepreneur links as well in order to stay on the safe side.

Money and when this is 'spent' or 'invested'

Paragraph 245D(c)(ii)(3) stipulates that funds will be considered as being 'invested' if they have been invested into a business or businesses, which the applicant is running as self-employed or as a director or as a member of a partnership. This means that if some of the funds are spent in another business, which either the applicant is not formally connected to or which is not relied upon for the purposes of claiming points in an application, these funds will not attract points in the 'investment' category.

An applicant's own remuneration is excluded as 'investment' under the same paragraph (245D(c)(ii)(1)) as well as the money spent to purchase a business from the previous owner (245D(c)(ii)(2)). The latter exclusion is worth re-producing in full as this can be tricky to assess sometimes depending on how creative the accounting is!

> *245D(c)(ii) 'Invested' means that the funds have been invested into a business or businesses which the applicant is running as self-employed or as a director or member of a partnership. 'Invested' or 'spent' excludes spending on:*

> *(1) (...)*
>
> *(2) buying any business from a previous owner, where the money ultimately goes to that previous owner (irrespective of whether it is received or held directly or indirectly by that previous owner) rather than into the business being purchased (This applies regardless of whether the money is channelled through the business en route to the previous owner, for example by means of the applicant or business purchasing 'goodwill' or other assets which were previously part of the business.)*

There are a number of applications where this exclusion would not have been applied as it was only introduced as an exclusion in the Immigration Rules later on. Therefore, it is worth checking when an applicant was initially granted the leave as a Tier 1 Entrepreneur and whether they are caught by this requirement at the extension stage.

Recently, the Upper Tribunal considered in *R (on the application of Anjum) v Entry Clearance Officer, Islamabad (entrepreneur – business expansion – fairness generally)* [2017] UKUT 00406 (IAC) the scenario of a proposal from a Tier 1 Entrepreneur applicant, who operated an existing business, to use part of his funds to purchase a second business for the purpose of developing and expanding the existing enterprise. The Upper Tribunal found that this was compatible with Paragraph 245 of the Immigration Rules and did not come under the exclusion set out at 245D(c)(ii)(2). The following extract is worth reproducing in full:

> "27. *Having considered these assorted provisions as a whole and in their full context, we are satisfied that where a Tier 1 applicant operates an existing business, the Rules do* <u>*not*</u> *prohibit the use of part of the minimum fund to purchase a second*

*business for the purpose of developing and expanding the existing enterprise. This represents, par excellence, investment in the Tier 1 business. It does not fall foul of the mischief of a smokescreen application which will involve investment of some or all of the minimum fund in something else. Nor does it encroach upon the related mischief of successive non-British business owners engaging in chain sales of the same business. On the contrary it is clearly harmonious with two of the identifiable underlying purposes of the Tier 1 scheme namely the promotion of the United Kingdom economy and the maintenance of properly regulated immigration control."*

It was arguably key in this case that the purchase of this second business formed part of the applicant's business proposal. It is important therefore to have these matters evidenced by way of a business plan or correspondence in order to substantiate an applicant's assertion that this is the nature and purpose of the investment, in full compliance with the Immigration Rules.

There are also a number of scenarios whereby spending is excluded for the purposes of assessing whether the spending can count as an 'investment':

- Spending is excluded if this is not directly for the purposes of establishing or running the applicant's own business(es) – paragraph (245D(c)(ii)(4)).

  It is important therefore to retain records of such spending, particularly if the spending is perhaps unusual or its purpose cannot be discerned at first glance. It may also be worth including a reference in the application to such spending and any necessary explanation and evidence.

- Spending is excluded if the money was invested more than 12 months (or 24 months if the applicant's previous leave was as a Tier 1 (Graduate Entrepreneur)) before the date of the application for initial leave as a Tier 1 Entrepreneur – paragraph 39(a)(iii) of Appendix A.

- Spending is excluded if money is invested in the form of a director's loan unless it is unsecured and subordinated to other creditors' loans to the business – paragraph 39(a)(iv) of Appendix A.

  In lay terms, this is when a director of the business, who may be the applicant, lends the company money. Such a loan needs to be unsecured, i.e. not secured by property or assets that become subject to seizure on default, and subordinated in favour of the other creditors' loans to the business. This means that the loan will only be repaid after all other creditors (not including the applicant) have been repaid.

- The Home Office will not award points for investments in any residential accommodation, property development or property management – paragraph 39(a)(v) of Appendix A.

  If in doubt, the Home Office guidance *Tier 1 (Entrepreneur)* - Version 21.0 is very helpful on this point and this restriction does not seek to exclude the construction and hotel industries nor decorating businesses and with some caveats, estate agent businesses:

  > *"This is because it is not the intention of this category to allow the applicant to set up as a landlord and let properties in the UK.*

*The intention is to promote UK competitiveness in business and to focus the investment on promoting business beneficial to the UK economy.*

*Property development is any development of property (real estate) owned by the applicant or their business to increase the value of this property with a view to earning a return either through rent or a future sale, or both.*

*Property management is the management of property, regardless of whether or not it is owned by the applicant or their business, for the purposes of renting it out or for resale.*

*An applicant is permitted to invest in:*

- *a company that is mainly involved in construction*
- *a decorating business if they do not own the property being improved*
- *a hotel, where the property is not being rented and guests don't sign a tenancy agreement*
- *an estate agency if they are not involved in letting the properties, or acting as landlords*

*The core principle is that the business income must be generated from the supply of goods and/or services, not from increased property values or from rent.*

*Applicants may not invest in student accommodation management services.*[2]"

2 p.70

# CHAPTER THREE
# HOW TO QUALIFY FOR TIER 1 (ENTREPRENEUR) LEAVE IN THE IMMIGRATION RULES

## FOR INITIAL LEAVE

As summarised in the first chapter, a successful applicant will be granted three years (three years and four months if granted entry clearance) of initial leave as a Tier 1 Entrepreneur.

It is important to refer to the first period of up to three years and four months as 'initial leave' as opposed to entry clearance or leave to remain. This is particularly so as the Tier 1 Entrepreneur route contains an unusual feature that an applicant can apply for an extension of leave by way of entry clearance. This aspect of the route will be covered in the third section of this chapter under *c. for the extension of leave.*

The requirements particular to applying for initial leave by way of entry clearance are set out at paragraphs 245DB (save for (i)-(j)) and 245DC of the Immigration Rules. The requirements for applying for initial leave by way of an in-country application are set out at paragraphs 245DD (save for (k)-(l)) and 245DE of the Immigration Rules.

There are numerous provisions seeking to restrict a person's ability to 'switch' into being a Tier 1 Entrepreneur if already residing in the UK in a different immigration category. These restrictions are set out at paragraph 245DD(e)-(f) of the Immigration Rules and should be checked before embarking on any in-country application for initial leave in this category.

On this note of 'switching', if seeking to switch in-country from being a Tier 1 (General) migrant or a Tier 4 (General) migrant, there are further requirements to contend with and these are set out at paragraph 36(b)-(c) and paragraph 44 of Appendix A. These provisions are not covered in any detail in this guide as they are very case specific and there are few of these cases remaining in the system.

There are also restrictions if seeking to apply for initial leave by way of entry clearance if the last leave of the applicant was as a Tier 4 (General) migrant and is being sponsored or was being sponsored by a government or international scholarship agency and that sponsorship ended 12 months ago or less. Unconditional written consent from the sponsoring body needs to be obtained and the specified documents stipulated at paragraph 245A need to be provided.

In order to be granted initial leave as a Tier 1 Entrepreneur, a total of 95 points need to be scored with 75 of these coming under the 'attributes' section contained in Appendix A. The other 20 points relate to the English language requirement and the availability of maintenance funds.

## Table 4 and the main requirements for applying for initial leave

Table 4 is the table to consult in Appendix A and sets out how the 75 points of attributes can be scored. Table 4 is reproduced here and provides the overview for applying for initial leave:

Table 4: Initial applications as referred to in paragraph 36

| Row | Investment and business activity | Points |
|---|---|---|
| 1 | (a) At least £200,000 is available to the applicant or their business, or has been invested in their business due to their activity, or<br><br>(b) At least £50,000 is available to the applicant or their business, or has been invested in their business due to their activity, from:<br><br>(i) one or more registered venture capital firms regulated by the Financial Conduct Authority (FCA),<br><br>(ii) one or more UK Entrepreneurial seed funding competitions listed as endorsed on the Department for International Trade pages of the GOV.UK website, or<br><br>(iii) one or more UK Government Departments, or Devolved Government Departments in Scotland, Wales or Northern Ireland, and made available by the Department(s) for the specific purpose of establishing or expanding a UK business, or<br><br>(c) At least £50,000 is available to the applicant or their business, or has been invested in their business due to their activity, and the applicant: | 25 |

| Row | Investment and business activity | Points |
|---|---|---|
| | (i) is applying for leave to remain, and<br><br>(ii) has, or was last granted, leave as a Tier 1 (Graduate Entrepreneur) Migrant. | |
| 2 | The money is held in one or more financial institutions, which are regulated by the appropriate regulatory body for the country in which they operate. | 25 |
| 3 | The money is disposable in the UK.<br>If the applicant is applying for leave to remain, the money must be held in the UK. | 25 |

As you will see, there is very little in the form of restriction if an applicant can show that they have access to £200,000. However, if the funds only amount to £50,000, the funding now has to be obtained from specific sources of funding, such as venture capital firms regulated by the Financial Conduct Authority, UK Entrepreneurial seed funding competitions endorsed by the Department for International Trade or UK/Devolved government funding. The exception to this is if the applicant's previous leave was a Tier 1 Graduate Entrepreneur. In these cases, applicants can rely on £50,000 of funding only and are not restricted as to the source of the funding either. Showing access to these funds will score 25 points.

Practitioners and applicants should be aware that the restrictions placed upon the £50,000 route were not always there. At its inception, £50,000 was the minimum and the funding source was not proscribed. It is important therefore to remember that there may still be applicants in the system, who will have been granted initial leave, for example, on the basis of their own funds amounting to £50,000.

A further two lots of 25 points are awarded to applicants provided the funds relied on are 1) held in one or more financial institutions, which are regulated by the appropriate body for the country in which they operate and 2) the funds are disposable in the UK. There is an added specification under the 'disposable' heading, which is if the applicant is applying for initial leave in-country. In those cases, the money must be held in the UK.

As well as needing to score a total of 75 points in Table 4, an applicant will need to satisfy the Home Office that they are a 'genuine' Entrepreneur or a 'genuine' prospective one. This requirement is set out at paragraph 245DB(f) and (h) when applying for initial leave by way of entry clearance and paragraph 245DD(h) and (j) if applying in-country. The 'genuineness' test and how this is applied in practice is looked at in detail in chapter four.

All applicants must then provide a business plan, setting out their proposed business activities in the UK and how they expect to make this business succeed, in support of their application (for entry clearance – paragraph 245DB(g) and in-country – paragraph 245DD(i)). There is no further guidance in either of the policy documents published by the Home Office as to what any business plan is expected to cover.

Applicants should be aware that their business plan forms a large part of their application and very often, this will be scrutinised by the Home Office. Applicants may wish to benefit from professional assistance when compiling their business plan but it is important for applicants to 'own' their business plan as it is they who will be quizzed on their business plan if interviewed by the Home Office and not the business consultant they may have employed.

The Home Office do also seem to have quite a basic and often over-simplistic understanding of business concepts and in particular, the market research that applicants are expected to have conducted. For instance, the Home Office does not appear to accept that an applicant may not have conducted any market research for their business proposal. This may be unusual for some business sectors, but for some businesses there may not be a need and very often business ventures develop organically and often by word-of-mouth. Even so, it is advisable to carry out as much market research as possible and to document this accordingly. Conversely, if none is carried out, applicants in these instances should make sure to justify their position and why it has not been necessary to undertake such research.

As is common with all PBS applications nowadays, the requirements set out above can be described as the substantive requirements, which an applicant will need to satisfy the Home Office of. However, there is a raft of evidential criteria, which applicants must also meet, and these are known as the 'specified evidence' requirements. It is important that practitioners, and applicants themselves, engage with these requirements meticulously and ensure that they are working from the most up to date version of the Immigration Rules. Within this guide, it is only possible to provide an overview of these requirements and so you should always double-check with the primary sources before finalising an application or advising a client on the same.

## For good measure, some more definitions

Before we come back to this evidential criteria, there are some further miscellaneous provisions or definitions contained in Appendix A, which you should be aware of when considering an application. Note that these provisions would also apply to the later stages in this route, i.e. to applications for further or indefinite leave to remain. These are as follows:

(i) An applicant will not get points if they are on the Companies House's list of disqualified directors [Paragraph 39(d) of Appendix A]

(ii) Evidence from an accountant submitted in support of an application can only be accepted if the accountant is not also the applicant and if the evidence meets the requirements of Paragraph 39(e) of Appendix A

(iii) Paragraph 39(f) of Appendix A stipulates several requirements concerning mainly the format of bank statements, whether personal or business ones.

In terms of miscellaneous provisions, which are specific to making an initial application and to showing access to the required funds, there are several stipulations contained in Paragraph 40 of Appendix A (taken slightly out of turn compared to the order in the Immigration Rules):

(i) An applicant can only qualify in one of three ways in Table 4, i.e. a) with access to £200,000 or b) with access to £50,000 from one or more venture capital firms, UK entrepreneurial seed funding competitions or UK/devolved government department funding or c) with access to

£50,000 as a Tier 1 (Graduate Entrepreneur). Neither can the sources of funding listed in b) be used in any other way but to qualify for the funding threshold in b) [Paragraph 40(f) of Appendix A].

(ii) An applicant can show the funds from different sources (e.g. from several bank accounts, combination of own and third party funds etc…) but there will be a need to collate and submit multiple documents in order to evidence the total amount of funds required on the same date [Paragraph 40(b) of Appendix A]

(iii) The funds need to be held in a UK regulated financial institution or they must be transferrable to the UK and convertible to sterling [Paragraph 40(c) of Appendix A] – this may cause difficulties for certain countries where there is a limit on the amount of currency that can be transferred out overseas.

(iv) Paragraph 40(g) of Appendix A defines when money is considered to be disposable in the UK and the tool to be used in order to convert foreign currencies is www.oanda.com using the date of the application.

(v) Paragraph 40(h) of Appendix A confirms that no points will be awarded where the funds are held in a financial institution for which the Home Office is unable to make satisfactory checks. Of course, 'satisfactory checks' are not defined in the Immigration Rules and you will need to request disclosure of the Home Office's checks if these are not forthcoming with any refusal. You are advised to make any financial institution aware that information and documentation relating to the account or funds held by the financial institution is being submitted to the Home Office for the purposes of an application so that they can assist as much as possible in case of any future contact from the Home Office.

(vi) If the funds are being made available to the business (as opposed to the applicant personally), then the business must be a company or a partnership and the applicant must be a director of the company or a partner in the partnership [Paragraph 40(d) of Appendix A with reference to specified evidence to that effect set out in Paragraph 42]

(vii) The funds must remain available until such time as they are 'spent' and note that the SSHD reserves the right to request further evidence to be satisfied of this or otherwise verify that the money will remain available and to refuse if evidence is not provided or cannot be satisfactorily verified [Paragraph 40(e) of Appendix A] – This also links into the provisions for curtailing leave, which are covered further below in this chapter in the third section under c) For the extension of leave.

Specified evidence

Returning to the specified evidence for initial applications and to show the funds are 'available', these are listed at Paragraph 41 of Appendix A. Since January 2018, there is now a useful table at Table 4A contained in the Immigration Rules, which is to be read in conjunction with Table 4. Table 4A sets out a convenient summary or check-list as to what categories of documentation an applicant will be required to produce in support of an application depending on the source of their funding, with cross-references to the relevant sub-paragraphs in Paragraph 41 of Appendix A.

When considering these provisions, you need to make note of terms such as *'all of'* or *'either/or as appropriate'* when determining whether it is necessary to include a certain piece of documentation. If in doubt, it is always best to submit the document in question with specific mention in a covering letter in order to guide the caseworker through the purpose of this piece of evidence.

When applying for initial leave, it is also possible to rely on funds, which have already been invested as long as these have been invested no earlier than in the last 12 months prior to making the application as a Tier 1 Entrepreneur. Whether the applicant has only invested some of the funds or the entirety of the funds required. The exception to this is if the applicant had prior leave as a Tier 1 Graduate Entrepreneur, in which case the relevant period for having already invested the entirety or some of the funds is 24 months, i.e. the duration of the leave as a Tier 1 Graduate Entrepreneur.

This is confirmed by Paragraph 43 of Appendix A with reference to Paragraph 45 and 48 of Appendix A making provision for the specified evidence concerning invested funds. Readers considering an application for initial leave where some or all of the funds have already been invested should also consult the third section of this chapter: *c) For the extension of leave.*

As part of an application for initial leave, all of the specified evidence requirements to show that funds are 'available' are contained in Paragraph 41 of Appendix A. This paragraph of the Rules covers all of the instances in which an applicant can have funds available, i.e. their own personal funds whether held in the UK or overseas, funds available to the applicant's business, seed funding competition or UK/Devolved Government Department funding, venture capital firm funding or third party funding. For the purposes of this guide, only the most common scenarios will be considered.

Third Party Funding

This is arguably the most problematic area of Tier 1 Entrepreneurial applications. Not only because a lot of applications seek to rely on third party funds but also because of some of the requirements stipulated at Paragraph 41.

The third party (or parties if there is more than one) making funds available to the applicant must sign a written declaration confirming that they have made the money available to invest in the applicant's business in the UK and this declaration must also contain the following information [Para 41(a)(vi)]:

- The names of the third party and applicant (an entrepreneurial team member where relevant) or the name of the applicant's business

- The date of the declaration

- The applicant's signature (and their team member where relevant) and the third party's signature

- The amount of money available in pounds sterling

- The relationship(s) of the third party to the applicant

- Further requirements if the third party is another business in which the applicant is self-employed or a director – see Para 41(a)(vi)(6)

- Confirmation that the money will remain available until such time as it is transferred to the applicant, the team or the applicant's business.

The main difficulty concerning the third party declarations is that applicants and their third party/parties may not reside in the same country. It is therefore unclear whether they need to both be present in order to sign this declaration together and neither pieces of guidance from the Home Office assist on this point.

As well as the written declaration, applicants seeking to rely on third party funding also need to provide a letter (or letters) from a legal representative(s), which confirm(s) *inter alia* that the written declaration(s) (covered above) and the letter(s) from institutions listed at paragraph 41(a)(ii)-(vi) and (viii) (covered below) contain the genuine signatures of the required signatories – Para 41(a)(vii). See also Paragraph 41(b)(7) for some further miscellaneous requirements).

Again, it is unclear how the legal representatives are expected to verify the genuineness of the signatures. This requirement does not stipulate that the legal representative must witness the applicant (and team member) and third party actually signing the written declaration. Presumably therefore, a reasonable check being conducted of the signatures on the written declarations against the signatory's passport or ID documentation should be sufficient but the better practice of witnessing the actual signature may be preferable just to be sure.

The rules have also been amended to confirm that the legal representative must be authorised to practice in the country where the third party or the money is as they are required to include in their letter the registration or authority confirming this. It was previously unclear what the Home Office expected in terms of legal representatives and applicants in the UK generally preferred to employ a legal representative practicing in this country. This is now only possible if the third party or the third party's funds are present in the UK.

It is even more unclear how the legal representatives are expected to verify the genuineness of the signatures on a financial institution's letter or documents emanating from a venture capital firm. It is hardly going to be likely that a bank is going to allow their customer's legal representative to be present when they sign their own letter although it may be worth a try. It may be possible to persuade the venture capital firm to do so but individual firms and financial institutions will operate differently.

One way to put into effect this requirement would be for the legal representative when writing their letter under Para 41(a)(vii) to confirm that they have considered the contents of, for example, the financial institution's letter and they are able to confirm that this institution has operated in the locality for 'x' number of years. They may also able to conduct enquiries of their own by, for instance, telephoning the authorised official from the financial institution, who signed the letter, to confirm the authenticity of the letter. A legal representative, who is authorised to practise in their own country, will be bound by a code of conduct and should be seen by the Home Office as acting in compliance with their duties not to mislead etc… Such confirmation should therefore be sufficient to comply with the wording contained in Paragraph 41(a)(vii).

This requirement to confirm the signatures in other letters and not just the third party funder's written declaration was only introduced into the Immigration Rules on 6th July 2018[1]. So it remains to be seen at the time of publishing how this provision will work in practice and more importantly, how it will be interpreted and enforced by the Home Office. It is also important to remember that this requirement will only apply to applications made on or after 6th July 2018, pursuant to the 'implementation' paragraph at p.2 of the Statement of Changes.

The third and final document that an applicant is required to submit when relying on third party funding is a letter from each financial institution holding the funds, i.e. the third party's funds which are being made available to the applicant or the applicant's business. This letter needs to confirm the amount of money that the third party intends to make available and that the institution is not aware of the third party having promised to make that money available to any other person [Paragraph 41(a)(viii)].

This is where applicants often encounter the most difficulties. As readers will no doubt be aware, a financial institution will often be cautious about committing matters to writing. Similarly, a bank acts upon its customer's instructions as long as these do not conflict with banking laws and practices. Many banks have therefore refused to comply with this requirement since, in their view, it is not within their remit to confirm what their customer 'intends' and may or may not 'promise'. The wording of this part of the Rule was even more problematic in older versions of the Immigration Rules and over time, the wording has softened somewhat. However, applicants are still encountering difficulties and the financial institution letters are often the cause of numerous refusals.

---

1 Statement of Changes published on 15 June 2018 HC 1154 §A5 p.18

As well as the requirements set out at Paragraph 41(a)(viii), the letter from third party's financial institution also needs to comply with the requirements set out at Paragraph 41(b). These requirements are common to certain letters mentioned in Paragraph 41, including the letters from the seed funding competition or UK/Devolved Government Department, from the venture capital firm and from the accountant confirming the financial condition of the venture capital firm's fund, from the legal representative confirming the signatures on the third party's written declaration and from any financial institution.

Thus, the third party funder's financial institution letter must also contain the following features:

- Be an original document and not a copy
- Be on official letter-headed paper
- Be dated no earlier than 31 days immediately before the date of application (different timescales apply for the other types of letters)
- State the applicant's name (team member where relevant) or the name of the applicant's business
- Include the contact details of the person or the official issuing the letter
- Include the name of the third party providing the money, including their full address, postal code, telephone contact number and any email address

- Show the account number

- Confirm that the financial institution is regulated by the appropriate body and if not regulated by the Financial Conduct Authority and the Prudential Regulation Authority that the money can be transferred in to the UK.

In keeping with the nature of 'specified evidence', if the third party's financial institution letter does not contain even just one of these stipulations, whether stipulated in Paragraph 41(a)(viii) or 41(b), the application is at risk of being refused. Readers should be mindful of the 'evidential flexibility' provisions contained in the Immigration Rules, which may provide some relief against such scenarios and which are covered in the last chapter of this guide. However, it is always best to ensure that the application does not fall foul of the requirements set out at Paragraph 41 in the first place rather than having to react to a concern raised by the Home Office further down the line.

The type of difficulties referred to above in the context of financial institution letters have in the past led to a raft of case-law being considered by the Immigration and Asylum Chamber of the Upper Tribunal and the Higher Courts. Sadly for applicants, none of the judgments are particularly helpful. They are worth considering in brief however as they may provide some tools to applicants and practitioners in order to convince the financial institutions concerned to issue the requested letters. Note that the wording of the Immigration Rules considered in the cases mentioned below has since been amended. The determinations and judgments need to be read in that context therefore but in many instances, some of the principles established still have application to date.

The first notable case to be reported by the Upper Tribunal is that of *Durrani (Entrepreneurs: bank letters; evidential flexibility)* [2014] UKUT 00295 (IAC). In these linked appeals, the appellants sought to argue that the requirements (then) contained in the Immigration Rules concerning the bank letters of third party funders should be construed other than literally in order to avoid absurd results. In these cases the banks were English ones and the appellants argued that the banks were not capable of providing such letters by reason of privity of contract and the relationship of confidentiality between bank and customer.

The appellants' arguments were rejected by the Upper Tribunal in a judgment given by the then-President Mr Justice McCloskey. The relevant part of the judicial head-note reads as follows [emphasis added]:

> (1) *The requirements listed in paragraph 41-SD(a)(i) of the Rules are to be construed reasonably and sensibly, in their full context. <u>Approached in this way, the letters required from banks or other financial institutions are not designed to provide, and do not commit them to, any form of guarantee or assurance to any party. Rather, the function of the prescribed letters is to attest to the state of the relevant bank account on the date when they are written and to provide certain other items of information designed to confirm the authenticity of the application for entrepreneurial migrant status and its economic viability. There is no difficulty in the third party bank, with its customer's consent, expressing its understanding, based on the customer's instructions, that the use of specified funds in the customer's bank account/s is contemplated or proposed by the customer for the purpose of financing the applicant's proposed business venture.</u> Accord-*

> *ingly, there is no substance in the argument that the relevant requirements contained in paragraph 41-SD(a)(i) produce an absurd result and must, therefore, be interpreted in some other manner.*

As readers can see, the Upper Tribunal made short shrift of the appellants' grounds of appeal enabling the Home Office's expectations of financial institutions in immigration cases to remain unchallenged. The underlined section of the head-note may still be useful however for applicants or practitioners to cite in a letter of instruction to the financial institution in question in order to try and provide them with some reassurance as to the purpose of the letter.

Later in 2015, the same type of issues and grounds of appeal were considered by the Court of Appeal in *Iqbal & others v Secretary of State for the Home Department* [2015] All ER (D) 54 (Mar), [2015] EWCA Civ 169. At Paragraph 18 of Sullivan LJ's judgment, the Upper Tribunal's determination in *Durrani* is explicitly approved. Further, in relation to one of the appeals before the Court, Sullivan LJ notes at Paragraph 26 of the judgment that *"(t)he fatal flaw in Mr Macdonald's submission is that there is no satisfactory evidence that the financial institutions referred to in Paragraph 41-SD(a)(i) would be unable or unwilling to provide the information required by that paragraph."*

Vos LJ added a short judgment of his own agreeing with that of Sullivan LJ. The following extracts reinforce the Court's view of the appellants' arguments but may also be helpful to cite to a financial institution as suggested above:

> *"31. One could have been forgiven for thinking, in listening to the argument in these cases which Sullivan LJ has recorded, that the term "purposive construction" was being used as shorthand for "convenient construction".*
>
> *(…)*
>
> *32. (…) (Mr MacDonal's) "purposive construction" enabled him to ignore the words actually used in the Rule, because he submitted that no bank could actually comply with that requirement. In my judgment, that is not an admissible approach.*
>
> *33. (…) I would hope that arguments of this kind will be less prevalent in future.*
>
> *34. In conclusion, I would wish to reiterate what Sullivan LJ has already intimated, namely that I know of no reason under English law why banks should not be prepared to write a letter confirming, if it be the case, that they have been instructed by their customer to provide the funds held in that customer's account for the benefit of a business enterprise being undertaken by a named applicant. As Bankes LJ explained in Tournier v National Provincial and Union Bank of England supra, a banker's implied duty of confidentiality does not apply where any disclosure is made with the consent of the customer."*

The arguments were, in my view, certainly worth running but ultimately unsuccessful. As mentioned above, the wording of the Immigration Rules has been since been changed but still presents the same type of difficulties for many applicants. Allowing time to liaise closely with the financial institutions is therefore essential and a letter from a legal representative to provide guidance and reassurance as per the above citations may also be worth considering. Lastly, if the financial institution concerned still refuses to issue the necessary letter and/or required information, it would also be advisable to obtain the institution's refusal or unwillingness to assist in writing.

## Venture Capital funding

Those seeking to rely on venture capital firm funding will need to obtain very comprehensive and specific evidence from the firm concerned. It is not sufficient anymore to present confirmation of the money being available from the venture capital firm [Para 41(a)(ii)(1)] but it is also necessary to provide a statement providing detailed information on the *"strategy, structure and financial exposure of the fund"* [Para 41(a)(ii)(2)], detailing *"the rationale for the investment, providing specific information about the circumstances which led to the investment decision"* [Para 41(a)(ii)(3)], and providing confirmation that the business/proposed business *"is a genuine and credible proposition"* [Para 41(a)(ii)(4)] and that the venture capital firm is registered with the Financial Conduct Authority as well as further details as to its entry on the register [Para 41(a)(ii)(5].

It is thought that these requirements were introduced in order to defeat venture capital firm 'factory applications'. When the Tier 1 Entrepreneur route was first introduced, it was not uncommon to see the same few venture capital firms support a high number of applications relying on the same type of business plans. As readers will see, the information that the venture capital firm's statement now needs to contain is very detailed and very specific to the applicant's proposed business venture.

In addition to the statement, the firm also needs to provide three further documents, which some might consider to be fairly onerous:

- A copy of the completed term sheet for the investment, signed by all parties to the transaction, including specified details at Paragraph 41(a)(iii).
- A breakdown of the technical, legal, commercial and financial due diligence conducted by the firm in support of the investment.
- A letter from an accountant validating the financial condition of the fund.

There is also plenty of room for the SSHD to take a different view on the genuineness and credibility of the proposed/business or the steps taken in relation to due diligence by the firm, so it is important to liaise closely with the venture capital firm in order to prepare this statement very carefully. The firm may not be experienced in dealing with the Home Office and so close communication and cooperation will often be necessary and should not be rushed.

Applicants should also ensure that there is sufficient time to enable this level of preparation before their application is due. It may also be that the venture capital fund is not willing to provide this level of information to the applicant or third parties. Applicants are advised therefore to familiarise themselves with these requirements at an early stage so that, if necessary, they can discuss these with the proposed venture capital firm in order to ascertain the feasibility of such funding and ultimately of preparing an application to the Home Office on this basis.

Before the rules were changed to reflect the above listed requirements, the case of *Arshad and others (Tier 1 applicants – funding – "availability": Pakistan)* [2016] UKUT 334 (IAC) was a case in point considered by the Upper Tribunal. The Tribunal linked several appeals together with the central common feature that each appellant had made a Tier 1 Entrepreneur application based on a representation that the entity known as Profectus Venture Capital would provide the funding of £50,000 required by the Immigration Rules. The Home Office had refused each application and found *"this funding scheme to be seriously flawed"* [Paragraph 6].

In considering the appeal, the Upper Tribunal reiterated that the onus of proving satisfaction of all of the material requirements of the Immigration Rules remains with every applicant. Specifically concerning the 'availability' of funds in the context of those provided by a venture capital firm as well as more widely, the judicial head-note contains the following guidance:

> *(iii) The Rules stipulate that every Tier 1 Entrepreneurial applicant have available £50,000 to invest in the proposed business venture. "Available" in this context denotes that the applicant must be in a position to invest this money in his business consequential upon a positive decision of the Secretary of State. The clear import of the Rules is that the investment must be capable of being made almost immediately thereafter.*
>
> (iv) *A mere intention on the part of a Tier 1 Entrepreneurial applicant to invest £25,000 at the outset of the business*

> *venture, coupled with a further intention to invest the balance of £25,000 at some unspecified future date from some unspecified source, does not satisfy the Rules.*

Applicant's own funds

The specified evidence for when an applicant is relying on their own funds is relatively more straight forward. The evidence differs depending on whether the funds are held overseas or in the UK. For overseas funds, an applicant is required to submit a letter from each financial institution holding the funds confirming the minimum balance available from the applicant's own funds held in that institution on the date of the letter. If an applicant has held the money for a consecutive 90-day period, the letter also needs to confirm this, with the period ending on the date of the letter [Para 41(a)(ix)]. Remember that all letters from financial institutions need to comply with the stipulations contained in Paragraph 41(b) of Appendix A, which were covered above in the context of third party funding.

For money held in the UK, it is a question of submitting the actual personal bank or building society statements, with the most recent statement being dated no earlier than 31 days before the date of application. Similarly, when it comes to bank statements Paragraph 39(f) should be borne in mind. The collection of statements, if there are several accounts being relied upon, need to show the total relevant sum of available money on the date of the most recent statement(s). Similarly, if held for a consecutive period of 90 days, the statements need to reflect this period immediately before the date of the statement [Para 41(a)(x)].

Money available to the applicant's business

Paragraph 42 covers applications where the money is available or being made available to the applicant's business, rather than to the applicant themselves. In these instances, an applicant must also provide a Companies House document showing the address of the business' registered office in the UK or head office in the UK if it has no registered office in the UK. The applicant also needs to show that he is a director, in the case of a company or a member in the case of a partnership.

## ENTREPRENEURIAL TEAMS

As mentioned in the first chapter, a major benefit of applying under this route of the PBS is that two applicants can group together and present their application for initial leave as a Tier 1 entrepreneurial team. This allows applicants, who may not have access to the full amount of funding on their own, to pool their resources with someone else and begin their business venture with a partner of their choice.

There are also disadvantages in that one team member may stand to be refused for completely different reasons, which may be separate to the Tier 1 entrepreneur business proposal, such as with a general ground of refusal relating to their past immigration history. If one team member is refused, this may obviously impact on the other team member's chances and may complicate matters further. Applicants wishing to consider this feature should therefore liaise closely with their potential team member and preferably seek legal advice so that all of the necessary information can be gathered by a set of representatives in order to maximise the assistance that can be provided. This of course may not be possible either at the outset or somewhere down the line in the cases of conflict of interest, but this is usually quite rare. The guidance that follows also applies to applications all the way through the Tier 1 Entrepreneur route and not just to initial leave applications.

Since January 2018, the rules concerning teams have been grouped together into two paragraphs at 52 and 53 of Appendix A. These are relatively self-explanatory and confirm that a team should only be comprised of two persons. Each person must have an equal level of control over the funds and, where relevant, equal status as owners, directors and/or members of the business or businesses in question [Para 52(a)]. The emphasis here is on the 'control'. This means that it does not matter that one member of the team is only contributing, for example, £50,000 out of the required £200,000 and the other team member is contributing the rest. This is an unequal share of the money being made available and ultimately invested. However, as long as the two team members have equal control of the entirety of the funds and, where relevant equal status as owners/directors or members, this would meet the requirements of the Immigration Rules.

To avoid the recycling of funds, an application will not be successful if an applicant has previously been granted leave as a Tier 1 Entrepreneur on the basis of investment or business activity when part of a team with someone else, if the same funds were relied on in a previous application. This does not prevent the same team of two applicants make several applications to the Home Office proposing to use the same funds if the first or indeed second application were not to be successful. It simply does not allow teams to re-form with different individuals when using the same sets of funds.

Similarly, Paragraph 53(c) stipulates that if an applicant is not the sole member or director of their business, they must provide confirmation of:

- The names of the other members or directors
- Whether any of the other members or directors are also Tier 1 Entrepreneurs
- If they are, the dates they became members or directors, whether they are applying under the provisions of Paragraph 52
- And if they have made (or are making at the same time) an application in which they claimed points for creating jobs, the names of the jobholders in question.

It is thought that Paragraph 53(c) is also intended to avoid the recycling of funds.

When it comes to entrepreneurial teams, there are also some more technical requirements to comply with:

- The team members need to be shown by name, passport number and, where relevant, PBS reference number in each other's applications and in the specified evidence required by Table 4/4A, 5 or 6 [Para 52(b)] – this is obviously to avoid confusion with applications from actual or potential team members and these being separated and treated differently by the Home Office, especially if each team member has a differing immigration history. Specific reference should also be made in the covering letter sent with the application and it helps to submit both applications at the same time if at all practicable.

- There are restrictions to consider at Paragraph 52 (a)(ii) if money is held by either of the team members in joint accounts with their respective spouse/partner if their spouse/partner is also a Tier 1 Entrepreneur or is applying to be so.

## FOR THE EXTENSION OF LEAVE

As summarised in the first chapter, a successful applicant when applying for an extension will be granted a further two years of leave. We will see that applications for an extension of leave all come under Table 5 in terms of the attributes and points awards in Appendix A. However, before we come to that, there is an interesting feature of this route, which is that an application can be made for an extension of leave as a Tier 1 Entrepreneur, once the initial minimum three-year period has been completed, from either the UK as an in-country application or from overseas as an entry clearance application. This is why I am using the term 'extension of leave' in this section as opposed to an 'extension of leave to remain'. I believe that this is the only route within the Immigration Rules where this is possible.

This feature is reflected in Paragraph 245DB of the Immigration Rules, which provides for the entry clearance requirements and where there is reference at (i) to an applicant having entry clearance, leave to enter or leave to remain as a Tier 1 Entrepreneur, or as having had such leave in the 12 months immediately before the date of the application and is being assessed under Table 5 of Appendix A. The requirements for applying for leave to remain, if applying in-country, and the references to Table 5 are then contained at 245DD(k).

The advantages of being able to apply for the extension of leave by way of entry clearance are that this may suit a particular applicant who travels a lot to their country of origin, perhaps as part of their business activity, and so this may tie in well as a matter of convenience. But it may also assist applicants who have had an application for an extension of leave already refused in-country and it is not possible to remedy any defects in that application within the period of 14 days under Paragraph 39E allowed as a grace period for overstaying by the Home Office. Such an applicant may prefer to leave the UK in order to make use of the 12 months from the date of their last leave as a Tier 1 Entrepreneur expiring and re-apply by way of entry clearance.

Any such applicant should make sure to seek legal advice prior to leaving the UK and prior to making such an application, as any further refusal may effectively amount to them being excluded from the UK for an indefinite period or at least until such time, within the timescales of 12 months, that their application is deemed to be successful by the entry clearance post. It is also worth considering that some entry clearance posts will have more experience of these types of applications than others.

It may be reasonable to expect that when applying for an extension of leave, having completed the initial three years in the same route and having presumably satisfied the genuineness test first time round, an applicant might be safe from this test from now on. This was indeed the case up until 19th November 2015. However, from this date, applications for an extension of leave and for ILR were also made subject to the 'genuineness' test. Applicants should therefore be mindful of this when preparing their application for an extension of leave and the fourth chapter of this guide covers these requirements in much more detail.

## Table 5 of Appendix A and the main requirements

As mentioned, Table 5 is the table to consult in Appendix A and sets out how the 75 points of attributes can be scored for an extension of leave application. Table 5 is reproduced here and provides the overview for applying for an extension of leave:

Table 5: Extension applications as referred to in paragraph 37

| Row | Investment, business activity and job creation | Points |
|---|---|---|
| 1 | The applicant has invested or has caused investment to be made by one or more third parties, totalling at least £200,000 (or £50,000 if they were awarded points for £50,000 funding or investment in their last grant of leave) in cash directly into one or more UK businesses.<br><br>The applicant does not need to provide evidence of this investment if they were awarded points under Table 5 in their last grant of entry clearance or leave to remain as a Tier 1 (Entrepreneur) Migrant. | 20 |
| 2 | The applicant has:<br><br>(a) registered with HM Revenue & Customs as self-employed, or | 20 |

| Row | Investment, business activity and job creation | Points |
|---|---|---|
| | (b) registered with Companies House as a director of a UK company, or member of a UK partnership.<br><br>The applicant must have registered as above within 6 months of entering the UK (if they were most recently granted entry clearance and there is evidence to establish their date of entry) or, in any other case, within 6 months of the date on which the most recent leave was granted. | |
| 3 | Within the three months before the date of application, the applicant was:<br><br>(a) registered with HM Revenue & Customs as self-employed, or<br><br>(b) registered with Companies House as a director of a UK company or member of a UK partnership. | 15 |
| 4 | The applicant has:<br><br>(a) established a new business or businesses that has or have created the equivalent of at least 2 new full time jobs for settled workers, or<br><br>(b) taken over or invested in an existing business or businesses and their services or investment have resulted in a net increase in the employment provided by the business or businesses for settled workers by creating the equivalent of at least 2 new full time jobs for settled workers. | 20 |

| Row | Investment, business activity and job creation | Points |
|---|---|---|
| | The jobs must have existed for at least 12 months during the applicant's most recent grant of leave as a Tier 1 (Entrepreneur) Migrant or, where that leave was granted less than 12 months ago, for at least the 12 months immediately before the date of application. | |

Applicants and practitioners should also be aware that it is possible to apply for ILR instead of an application for an extension under the 'accelerated ILR route' if a certain criterion is met. The criterion is quite onerous but it is open to applicants to apply for ILR after having resided in the UK for a period of three years only as a Tier 1 Entrepreneur. The criteria and application procedure are looked at more closely at the end of the ILR section of this chapter below.

As you can see, there are two major requirements to fulfil by the time applicants come to apply for an extension of leave. The first is they need to have effected the investments, or caused the investments to be made by one or more third parties, amounting to the entirety of the funds that they qualified for when granted the initial leave, i.e. either amounting to £50,000 or £200,000. The investments need to have been made in cash directly into one or more UK businesses [Row 1].

If an applicant was already awarded points when applying for initial leave for having invested some or the entirety of the funds at that stage, such an applicant does not need to provide the evidence of the investments again at the extension of leave stage. A mention of this in a covering letter would be worth considering however.

The second major requirement is to have established a new business or businesses and have created the equivalent of at least 2 new full-time jobs for settled workers. If taking over or investing in an existing business or businesses, the new jobs need to represent a net increase in the employment provided by the business(es) for settled workers. The jobs must have also existed for a period of at least 12 months during the applicant's most recent grant of leave as a Tier 1 Entrepreneur [Row 4].

There are two further and more technical requirements:

- Row 2: Within six months of entering the UK (if they were previously granted entry clearance and there is evidence of their date of entry) or within six months of the date on which their most recent leave was granted, the applicant has registered with HMRC as self-employed or registered with Companies House as a director of a UK company or a member of a UK partnership.

- Row 3: Within the three months before the date of the application for an extension of leave, the applicant was registered with HMRC as self-employed or with Companies House as a director of a UK company or a member of a UK partnership.

It may seem at first glance a bit excessive to have to show evidence of these registrations at two different points in time. However, this is to show the continuity of an applicant's business activity but also to cover instances whereby, for example, an applicant may have started one business model shortly after starting their journey as a Tier 1 Entrepreneur with being registered as a self-employed, only for this business venture to fail and be abandoned at a later date. As long as this same applicant started a new business or took over an existing one within the duration of their leave and fulfilled the investments and job creation requirements, they will be able to show that they were registered with HMRC as self-employed or with Companies House in the other capacities at both points in time: i.e. within six months of their entry/initial grant of leave and within the three-month period prior to the date of their application for an extension of leave. The Home Office accepts that some business plans will fail or never come to full fruition but thankfully this does not necessarily entail the end of an applicant's Tier 1 journey as an entrepreneur. As long as applicants remain active, resilient and determined that is!

Curtailment

Before considering the specified evidence attached to the requirements summarised above, applicants should be made aware that there are specific provisions contained in Paragraph 245DE of the Immigration Rules for the curtailment of leave, which are *"without prejudice to the grounds for curtailment in Paragraph 323"* of Part 9 of the Immigration Rules covering the general grounds for refusal.

The curtailment provisions contained in Paragraph 245DB(c) are discretionary in nature and apply to curtailing leave to enter or remain – see the words *"may be curtailed"* – and are limited to the following instances:

- If an applicant has not registered with HMRC as self-employed or not registered a new company or partnership in which he is a director or partner or not registered as a director or member of an existing business or partnership [Para 245DE(c)(i)(1)-(3)].

- If the funds previously relied upon as being available for the purpose of investments cease to be available to the applicant, except where they have been spent for the purposes of the business(es) [Para 245DE(c)(ii)].

Applicants need to have carried out the relevant tasks set out in the first bullet point by the same date as referred to in Row 2 of Table 5 and this is explicitly set out again at Paragraph 245DE(d)(i)-(iii) for the avoidance of doubt.

It is difficult to see how the Home Office would ordinarily come to notice that an applicant has failed to register themselves or their business in the ways set out at Paragraph 245DE(c)(i) but as we know, the Home Office have the power to make enquiries and it is often in the context of other immigration enforcement duties that these checks and curtailment decisions arise. In relation to the funds ceasing to be available, this may arise if a third party funder had a falling out with an applicant and subsequently notified the Home Office or if a third party funder business closed down and this came to the attention of the Home Office.

Specified evidence

Unfortunately, the same type of over-proscribed requirements exist when it comes to the specified evidence in the context of the investment of funds. It cannot be reiterated enough how much an applicant needs to familiarise themselves with the requirements of the Immigration Rules as they progress through their Tier 1 Entrepreneur journey. It is almost a case of an applicant needing to run their business, administratively at least, in such a way that will generate the type and format of documents capable of keeping the Home Office happy.

Paragraph 45 of Appendix A contains all of the requirements relating to specified documents on investments. The type of documents that need to be submitted will depend on how the investments were made. However, applicants need to be aware that it is not sufficient to submit, for example, a set of business or financial accounts when required to do so as the content of such accounts is also 'specified'. Certain aspects of the specified evidence seem to be driven by the Home Office and would not necessarily be compiled in the way that is stipulated in the Immigration Rules in the course of ordinary business administration and management.

Business/financial accounts

All applicants applying for an extension of leave must provide their business accounts *"and accompanying evidence of their investment, which must meet the (...) requirements"* set out at Paragraph 45. If the business is legally required to produce audited accounts, then audited accounts must be submitted to the Home Office in support of the application [Para 45(a)]. If the business is not legally required to produce audited accounts, then unaudited accounts will obviously suffice together with an accounts compilation report from an accountant [Para 45(b)].

At Paragraph 45(f), further requirements are stipulated which relate to the content of the business accounts. These must clearly show the name of the accountant, the date on which the accounts were produced, and how much the applicant has invested in the business.

The part that often leads to many refusals of application resides in Paragraph 45(c), which states that the accounts (whether audited or unaudited) must show the investment in money made directly in the business by:

- The applicant, in their own name; or
- One or more seed funding competitions or UK/Devolved Government Departments with the accounts being accompanied by a letter from the source, confirming that the investment was made on the applicant's behalf; or
- A third party (other than above) and the accounts must either:
    (1) Confirm that the investment was made as a result of the applicant's activity, or

    (2) Be accompanied by a letter from the Department for International Trade, confirming that the investment was made as a result of the applicant's activity.

The last bullet point [Para 45(c)(iii)] is slightly confusing in my view. The Home Office guidance is however quite helpful:

> *"If the applicant's business has an existing support relationship with DIT, investment can be shown in the accounts as being made in the name of the investing entity. Where this is the case the financial accounts must be supplemented by a letter from DIT confirming that this investment was made on the applicant's behalf, for the purposes of compliance with the rules. This only applies if the source of funds is not:*

- *one or more UK seed funding competitions listed as endorsed on the Department for International Trade pages of the GOV.UK website*

- *one or more UK government departments or devolved government departments in Scotland, Wales or Northern Ireland"*[2]

It is also to be noted that paragraph 45(c)(iii) (paraphrased in the last bullet point above) was amended to come into force on 6th July 2018 with the same Statement of Changes[3], which amended the requirement for legal representatives' letters confirming the genuine signatures in letters from financial institutions and venture capital firms. Similarly, this change only applies to applications made on or after 6th July 2018.

In my experience, many sets of accounts will not detail the name of the source of the investment, whether it is the applicant's or another of the agencies referred to above. It is possible to get accounts amended and then re-filed with Companies House in order to rectify these difficulties but it is advisable to liaise closely with the business' accountant in the first place in order to avoid any difficulties arising out of this requirement.

Director's loans

Another way of effecting the investment(s) are by way of a director's loan – Paragraph 45(d). If this is the case, there are three types of documents that need to be collated and submitted:

---

2 Tier 1 (Entrepreneur) Version 21.0, published 16 January 2018 p.93

3 Statement of changes HC 1154 §A6 p.18

(i) The business' accounts for the relevant period which need to show the director's loan(s),

(ii) The applicant's business bank statements, which must show the investments being made through readily identifiable transactions and which must clearly show the transfer of this money from the applicant to their business, and

(iii) A legal agreement between the applicant and the business showing the terms of the loan, any interest that is payable, the period of the loan and that the loan is unsecured and subordinated to other creditors' loans to the business.

Again, the most frequently problematic requirement is (ii). What an applicant may view as 'readily identifiable transactions' may not be so to the Home Office. If an applicant has transferred their own funds from their personal bank account(s) to their business one(s) in order to effect the director's loan and ultimately the investment, then it would usually be necessary to submit both sets of bank statements, personal and business. Surprisingly, this is often not done but in fairness, Paragraph 45(d)(ii) only refers to business bank statements.

It is thus advisable to follow the lead provided by the words *"and accompanying evidence of their investment"* at the start of Paragraph 45 and to submit all of the documentation that is thought necessary to complete the paper trail between the money leaving the funding source and reaching the business by way of investments. This requirement of *"readily identifiable transactions"* only applies to investments made after 19$^{th}$ November 2015, which is when this provision was brought into force.

Other ways of effecting the investments

Paragraph 45(e) lists the documents that need to be submitted if the applicant has made the investment in the form of share capital. Again, this relates back to the accounts, which must show the shareholders, the amount and value of the shares (on date of purchase) in the applicant's name. Applicants can also provide a printout of the company's register of members from Companies House if the value of the applicant's share capital is not shown in the accounts.

If investing via a venture capital firm, Paragraph 45(g) confirms that an original and dated letter from the firm on its headed paper suffices, which details the applicant's name, the date(s) the money was transferred to the applicant or invested in their business and that the firm was registered with the FCA on the date(s) of the relevant transfer(s). There is also a further requirement, which is dealt with immediately below.

Lastly, if the investments have been via seed funding competition, UK/Devolved Government Department funding or venture capital firm and the points for investments have not already been awarded to the applicant as part of a previous application, the specified evidence listed in Table 4A as evidence of the source of the funds also needs to be submitted except that the letters referred to in Paragraph 41(a)(i) and (ii) do not need to be dated within the three months immediately before the date of the application.

Investments in property

Readers will recall the restrictions placed by the route generally on establishing businesses in the field of property development and/or management (Paragraph 39(a)(v) of Appendix A covered in the second chapter). A further reference to this restriction can be found at Paragraph 45(i): if an applicant has purchased property as part of their business investment. This rule confirms that the value of any residential accommodation cannot be included towards the value of the investment made.

In these instances, applicants will need to provide an estimate of the value of the residential accommodation if it is part of the premises also used for the business. The said valuation must also be from a surveyor who is a member of the Royal Institution of Chartered Surveyors and dated within the three months before the date of the application. A common scenario where this would need to be considered is the purchase of a shop or office at street level with a residential property on the first floor.

## Job creations and the key definitions

Paragraph 49 of Appendix A sets out the definitions applied by the Home Office as to what amounts to a 'job' and further defines what can count towards the 12 months of the job's existence.

Essentially, a full-time job must consist of at least 30 hours of paid work per week [Para 49(a)] and must comply with all relevant UK legislation including, but not limited to, the national Minimum Wage Regulations in effect at the time and the Working Time Regulations 1998 [Para 49(g)]. However, each of the two jobs can be combined from two or more part-time jobs as long as these combinations add up to 30 hours per week and each job (as a sum of the part-time workers where relevant) has existed for 12 months. For obvious reasons, each employee being relied upon as part of a job 'combination' must be clearly identified by the applicant in their application [Para 49(f)].

The Home Office also clarified through Paragraph 49(b) that one full time job of more than 30 hours of work per week will not count as more than one full time job. Paragraph 49(e) does also confirm that different jobs that have existed for less than 12 months cannot be combined together to make up a 12-month job. There is an exception to this for applicants, who successfully applied for their initial leave before 6th April 2014 (when this restriction did not exist), have had continuous leave since then and their application for entry clearance, leave to remain or indefinite leave to remain is made before 6th April 2019.

Usefully, Paragraph 49(c) also clarifies that the 12 months period of existence does not have to be a consecutive set of 12 months provided that it is the same job. The example of lasting for 6 months in one year and then 6 months the following year is given. This may suit businesses, which may not have a steady work-flow but may require short-term staff to cover certain projects over the course of a year or so.

At Paragraph 49(d), it is confirmed that the jobs do not need to be in existence still at the time of the application for an extension of leave as long as the 12 months period was fulfilled prior to the application. We will also see that this also applies to application for indefinite leave to remain as long as a further 12 months period of job creation was completed by the applicant whilst progressing through their extension of leave.

Job creation and specified documents

The specified documents to submit in order to evidence the job creations are set out at Paragraph 50. It is best for applicants and practitioners to consult this paragraph in full as there are a high number of documents to submit, such as Real Time Full Payment

Submissions, duplicate payslips, employee nationality or immigration status documents etc.... This is due to the documents needing to evidence several aspects of the job creations:

- That two full-time jobs or their equivalent were created and the number of hours per week is met,
- That the wage or salary payments complied with PAYE reporting requirements throughout the full period of employment used to claim the points,
- Confirmation of the employment start date(s), hours paid per pay period and the hourly rate for each settled worker relied upon, including any changes to the same and the dates of those changes,
- Copies of the necessary documents to evidence the settled status of the employees concerned.

Depending on the applicant's status in the business, i.e. whether they are self-employed [Para 50(e)] or a director or a member of a partnership [Para 50(f)], there are further documents to submit to show their respective status at the time the employees were employed and in the case of self-employed applicants, the bank statements referred to in Paragraph 48(a)(iii) (covered below) also need to show all of the payments made to the employee in the full period of employment used to claim points as well as the address of the business [Para 50(e)].

If an applicant took over an existing business or joined an existing business, as mentioned in Table 5, the job creations need to represent a net increase in the business' employment of staff, regardless of how long the business existed for before the applicant took this over or joined it.

In order to evidence this net increase, applicants will therefore need to comply with Paragraph 50(g)-(h) and submit an original, signed and dated letter from an accountant, effectively detailing the position of the business prior to the applicant taking it over or joining and the position thereafter and dealing with each point raised in Paragraph 50(g). In instances where the business did employ workers prior to the applicant's involvement in the business, the accountant's letter also needs to be accompanied by one year's Real Time Full Payment Submissions sent to HMRC, or if the business was reporting before Real Time a form P35, for the year prior to the applicant's involvement.

Through a combination of these documents, the Home Office should in theory have the full picture of a business established by the applicant for the first time and how it progressed to creating two full-time jobs for settled workers or a business which was taken over or joined by the applicant and where there has been a net increase in employment by two full-time jobs. The latter being with the 'before' and 'after' sets of documents.

*Business activity and the various evidence of an applicant's registrations with HMRC and/or Companies House*

I have covered this part of Table 5 last as there is less room for differing interpretations and less definitions to cover when looking at the evidence an applicant needs to submit to demonstrate their various registrations as self-employed, as a director or as a member of a partnership.

The requirements are listed at Paragraphs 47 and 48 of Appendix A and are fairly self-explanatory. They also apply to Table 6 for applications for indefinite leave to remain. Essentially, if an applicant registered as self-employed within the six-month period referred to in Tables 5 and 6, evidence of this registration with HMRC needs to be submitted. In the case of a director or a member of a partnership, the same but from Companies House in the form of a printout of the company's filing history page and of the applicant's personal appointments history showing the date of their appointment [Para 47].

The same type of evidence also needs to be submitted to show that an applicant has been engaged in business in the UK when they are making their application. So if self-employed [Para 48(a)(i)-(iii)], evidence (dated no earlier than three months before the date of the application) of their HMRC registration to show that their business is based in the UK, HMRC evidence that the applicant is submitting self-assessment tax returns and a personal bank statement showing transactions for their business or business bank statements or a letter from their financial institution in the UK confirming that the applicant has a business and acts through that bank for the purpose of that business.

Similarly, if a director or a member of a partnership, such applicants need to submit printouts from Companies House, also dated no earlier than three months before the date of the application, showing all of the following [Para 48(b)(i)(1)-(4)]:

- The address of the registered office in the UK, or head office in the UK if it has no registered office,
- The applicant's name, as a director or member

- The date of the applicant's appointment as a director or member, and

- The business is actively trading (not dormant, struck-off, dissolved or in liquidation),

Director or partner applicants also need to submit evidence from HMRC confirming that the company is registered for corporation tax (if the applicant is a director of a company) and a business bank statement from a UK account which shows business transactions, or a letter from the UK bank in question, on its headed paper, confirming that the company or partnership has a bank account, that the applicant is a signatory of that account, and that the company or partnership uses that account for the purposes of their business [Para 48(b)(ii)-(iii)].

There will obviously be an overlap between the documents collated and submitted in compliance with Paragraph 48 and those obtained pursuant to Paragraph 49. However, it is important to ensure that all of these documents are obtained regardless of any overlap or repetition since it is the two points in time that differ and that are important to demonstrate in order to satisfy the requirements listed at Rows 2 and 3 of Table 5 (i.e. six months post-entry/leave granted *vs* three months prior to the application for an extension of leave).

## FOR INDEFINITE LEAVE TO REMAIN

The requirements for applying for indefinite leave to remain ('ILR') are set out at Paragraph 245DF with reference to Table 6 in Appendix A. The same general grounds of refusal [Para 245DF(b) and (e)] and common criteria to all application, such as the English language requirement [Para 245DF(d)], apply and an applicant must score another set of 75 points in Attributes.

As was the case with extension applications, the 'genuineness' test was also introduced for ILR applications albeit at a later stage than when this was first introduced for initial leave applications [Para 245DF(f)-(k)] and this is covered in more detail in Chapter 4.

Table 6 and the main requirements for applying for ILR

Table 6 in Appendix A provides as follows:

Table 6: Applications for indefinite leave to remain as referred to in paragraph 38

| Row | Investment, business activity and job creation | Points |
|---|---|---|
| 1 | The applicant has invested or has caused investment to be made by one or more third parties, totalling at least £200,000 (or £50,000 if they were awarded points for £50,000 funding or investment in their last grant of leave) in cash directly into one or more UK businesses. | 20 |

| Row | Investment, business activity and job creation | Points |
|---|---|---|
| | The applicant does not need to provide evidence of this investment if they were last granted entry clearance or leave to remain as a Tier 1 (Entrepreneur) Migrant, having been awarded points under Table 5. | |
| 2 | The applicant was:<br><br>(a) registered with HM Revenue & Customs as self-employed, or<br><br>(b) registered with Companies House as a director of a UK company or member of a UK partnership.<br><br>The above requirement must have been met:<br><br>(i) within 6 months of entering the UK (if they were most recently granted entry clearance and there is evidence to establish their date of entry) or, in any other case, within 6 months from the date the most recent leave was granted, and<br><br>(ii) within the three months before the date of application.<br><br>The applicant does not need to provide evidence of (i) if they were last granted entry clearance or leave to remain as a Tier 1 (Entrepreneur) Migrant, having been awarded points under Table 5. | 20 |

| Row | Investment, business activity and job creation | Points |
|---|---|---|
| 3 | The applicant has:<br><br>(a) established a new business or businesses that has or have created the equivalent of at least 2 new full time jobs for settled workers, or<br><br>(b) taken over or invested in an existing business or businesses and their services or investment have resulted in a net increase in the employment provided by the business or businesses for settled workers by creating the equivalent of at least 2 new full time jobs for settled workers.<br><br>The jobs must have existed for at least 12 months during the applicant's most recent grant of leave or, where that leave was granted less than 12 months ago, for at least the 12 months immediately before the date of application. | 20 |
| 4 | (a) The applicant has spent a continuous period of 5 years lawfully in the UK with leave as a Tier 1 (Entrepreneur) Migrant, or<br><br>(b) The applicant has spent a continuous period of 3 years lawfully in the UK as a Tier 1 (Entrepreneur) Migrant, and has:<br><br>(i) created the equivalent of at least 10 (including the two jobs already relied upon to score points under row 3) new full time jobs which meet the requirements in row 3 above, or | 15 |

| Row | Investment, business activity and job creation | Points |
|---|---|---|
| | (ii) established a new UK business or businesses that has or have had a gross income from business activity of at least £5 million during the 3 year continuous period, or<br><br>(iii) taken over or invested in an existing UK business or businesses and the applicant's services or investment have resulted in a net increase in gross income from business activity of £5 million during the 3 year continuous period, when compared to the 3 year period immediately before the date the applicant became involved with the business. | |

By this stage in an applicant's Tier 1 Entrepreneur journey, a lot of the requirements listed in Table 6 should have been met within the previous application stages. For instance, Row 1 confirms that evidence of the investments does not need to be provided again if the applicant was previously awarded points under Table 5. Oddly though, I cannot think of a scenario whereby an applicant would qualify to apply for ILR not having scored the necessary points at the extension stage under Table 5.

Similarly, an applicant does not need to evidence their relevant registrations with either HMRC or Companies House, depending on their status in the business, at the six months entry stage [Table 6 Row 2 (i) with reference to (a) or (b)] since this will have also been done under Table 5 when previously applying and being granted an extension of leave. All that is required under Table 6 is to continue to show that the applicant remains either registered with HMRC as self-employed or with Companies House as a director or member of a partnership [Row 2 (ii) with reference to (a) or (b)]. In order to satisfy this requirement again, it is the same specified evidence that is listed at Paragraph 48 of Appendix A that needs to be collated and submitted and which we covered above under 'business activity' in the 'extension of leave' section.

The last main requirement to meet is that of job creations again and so readers are referred to the 'job creations' in the 'extension of leave' section as it is the same requirements that apply again and Paragraphs 49 and 50 of Appendix A should be consulted again. As mentioned in that section, the evidence that will need to be submitted at the ILR stage will very much depend on whether the jobs that were created while the applicant progressed through their initial leave were still in existence for a duration of 12 months while the applicant held the extension of leave. As confirmed by Paragraph 49(d), the jobs do not need to exist at the time of the application, whether under Table 5 for an extension of leave or under Table 6 for ILR. However, the jobs need to have existed for a period of 12 months during each stint of leave – so to speak.

If the jobs are the same throughout, it is still advisable to submit all of the documentation again in instances where an applicant took over or joined an existing business in order to show the net increase in employment. This is because there is no note at Row 3 to confirm that an applicant need not re-submit evidence which was submitted at the previous stage and which attracted the award of points. In any event, an applicant requesting ILR will need to show that the same jobs continued to exist for a further 12-month period and so this aspect of the evidence will be new to the Home Office and Paragraph 50 needs to be complied with again.

If the jobs are different, the evidence will be also be different so this should be submitted in full in order to comply with Paragraph 50. Readers are again referred to the 'jobs creation' section above as it is the same criteria that apply in ILR applications.

Accelerated ILR route

In addition to the other criteria, Row 4 of Table 6 confirms that ILR will be granted if an applicant has spent a continuous period of 5 years lawfully in the UK with leave as a Tier 1 Entrepreneur. However, as mentioned briefly in the 'extension of leave' section above, Row 4 also allows for applicants to apply for ILR under an 'accelerated route' if at least one of two criteria are met and a continuous period of three years has been spent in the UK lawfully as a Tier 1 Entrepreneur.

The two possible criteria are:

- If the applicant has created the equivalent of at least ten new full-time jobs which meet the requirements in Row 3 on job creations. The ten new jobs are inclusive of the two jobs referred to in Row 3 [Row 4(b)(i) of Table 6], or

- If the applicant has established a new UK business or businesses that has/have had a gross income from business activity of at least £5 million during the three-year continuous period. This also applies to business(es) that the applicant has taken over or joined, and the applicant's involvement has resulted in a next increase in gross income from business activity of £5 million during the three year continuous period, when compared to the three year period immediately before the date the applicant became involved with the business [Row 4(b)(ii)-(iii) of Table 6].

Paragraph 51 of Appendix A provides for the specified documents if applying under the accelerated route. It is relatively straight forward if the applicant has established a new business or businesses and is relying on the gross income of £5 million criteria as all that is needed to submit are the audited or unaudited account which show the gross income resulting from the business' activities and that this reached the required income.

It is more onerous documents-wise if the applicant has taken over or joined an existing business. The documents required are listed at Paragraph 51(b) and include the sets of accounts for the three-year period prior to and post the applicant's involvement showing the net increase. The accounts also need to show the name of the accountant and the date the accounts were produced, which would usually be the case in any event [Para 51(b)(i)(1)-(4)]. Applicants in these instances also need to submit an original, signed and dated letter from an accountant confirming the name and contact details of the business, an explanation of the applicant's status in the business, the net increase in the business activity, the registration or permission of the accountant to operate in the UK and that the accountant will verify the content of the letter to the Home Office on request [Para 51(b)(ii)(1)-(5)]. Paragraph 39(e) of Appendix A should also be consulted for good measure.

Paragraph 51 does not detail the specified documents needed if the applicant wishes to apply for accelerated ILR under the second criteria of 10 job creations. This is because it is the same specified evidence that is required for all job creations and which can be found at Paragraph 49 and 50. Applicants and practitioners should be doubly cautious when preparing ILR applications on this basis since the evidence to demonstrate the creation of ten jobs will be hugely voluminous. It was already so with two jobs and will be even more so if the applicant has taken over or joined an existing business or businesses as the net increase will need to be shown.

In my experience, these applications have a fairly high refusal rate for the simple reason that a document or several are either missed in the preparation stage of the application or missed by the Home Office. It cannot be reiterated enough that a very skilled and detailed covering letter should be included with all such applications in order to guide the Home Office through the documentation but also to act as a check-list for the application or their legal representative and finally as evidence that the required documentation was submitted in support of the application in case a challenge needs to be brought against any refusal further down the line.

One would have thought that the Home Office may treat these applications more sympathetically if a document is missing in light of the potential benefits to the UK of business(es) reaching £5 million in gross income and/or employing at least ten settled workers, but this does not appear to be the case. I have had experience of applications being refused due to some documents allegedly not being submitted, the same applicants were subsequently threatened with removal and detained only to be later released and granted ILR upon a reconsideration of their application, which only followed after the lodging of a judicial review claim.

# CHAPTER FOUR THE GENUINENESS TEST

Having considered the main concepts to the Tier 1 Entrepreneur route in the second chapter as well as the more technical and substantial requirements of each stage of the Tier 1 Entrepreneur journey including the minefield of 'specified evidence' in the third chapter, we will now take a closer look at the 'genuineness' test.

The requirement to satisfy the Secretary of State and Home Office case-workers of an applicant's credibility has not always been in existence. Practitioners may be aware that the whole purpose of the PBS was seemingly to take discretion out of the equation and to try and stick to a transparent and easier to understand system of points award. Previous rules, which were designed to test an applicant's intention to do something, such as an intention to study a particular course or not to take employment up outside of that allowed by a certain category of leave's condition. The Green Paper, which introduced the system, "*A points-based system: making migration work for Britain*" highlighted the following:

> *"Applicants will find the system simpler to understand and the rules for entry clearer and more consistently applied. It will be quicker and simpler for employers and educational institutions to bring in the migrants they need, and there will be more certainty about whether prospective migrants will be able to come to the UK. The public will better be able to understand who we are allowing into the UK and why, and have confidence that the system is not being*

> *abused. It will also be more straightforward for entry clearance officers and caseworkers to administer."*[1]

Within the Tier 1 Entrepreneur route, the 'genuine' entrepreneur test was first introduced in 2013. It was only introduced for initial applications at first and this changed from 6th April 2015, when it was extended to extension and ILR applications.

The Migration Advisory Committee's *"Review of the Tier 1 Entrepreneur and Graduate Entrepreneur routes"* published in September 2015 noted that:

> *"It is likely that the introduction of the genuine entrepreneur test has been a contributing factor in the rise in Tier 1 (Entrepreneur) application refusal rates which rose from 36 per cent in 2012 to 49 per cent in 2014 for in-country applications and for out-of-country applicants rose from 21 percent in 2012 to 44 per cent in 2014."*[2]

This test has had a huge impact on applications and as we will see in the next chapter, with the statutory appeals falling away, the means to challenge a refusal of an application on genuineness grounds have become very limited. Let us first look at what the

1 Home Office, *A points–based system: making migration work for Britain,* Cm 6741, March 2006, p.1 - https://assets.publishing.service.gov.uk/government/uploads/system/uploads/attachment_data/file/272243/6741.pdf

2 Paragraph 4.40 - https://assets.publishing.service.gov.uk/government/uploads/system/uploads/attachment_data/file/472236/Report_Tier_1_Entrepreneurs.pdf

Immigration Rules actually say and how the Home Office is to assess an applicant's credibility.

## THE IMMIGRATION RULES AND HOW THE HOME OFFICE ASSESSES AN APPLICANT'S GENUINENESS

The criteria and what the Home Office will take into consideration is set out in the Immigration Rules for each stage of the Tier 1 Entrepreneur route. For the initial leave, this is at Paragraphs 245DB(f) and (h) if applying by way of entry clearance or Paragraph 245DD(h) and (j) if applying in-country. The requirements at 245DB(f) and 245DD(h) state the following:

(1) The Applicant genuinely intends and is able to establish, take over or become a director of one of more businesses in the UK within the next six months;

(2) The applicant genuinely intends to invest the money referred to in Table 4 of Appendix A in the business(es) referred to above;

(3) That the money referred to in Table 4 is genuinely available to the applicant and will remain available to him until such time as it is spent for the purposes of his business(es);

(4) If the applicant is relying on one or more previous investments to score points, they have genuinely invested all or part of the investment funds required in Table 4 into one or more genuine businesses in the UK;

(5) The applicant does not intend to take employment in the United Kingdom other than under the terms of paragraph 245DC.

At Paragraph 245DB(h) and 245DD(j), the Home Office set out what the decision-maker will take into account when assessing on the balance of probabilities the applicant's 'genuineness'. The list of factors is as follows:

(6) The evidence the applicant has submitted;

(7) The viability and credibility of the source of the money referred to in Table 4 of Appendix A;

(8) The viability and credibility of the applicant's business plans and market research into their chosen business sector;

(9) The applicant's previous educational and business experience (or lack thereof);

(10) The applicant's immigration history and previous activity in the UK; and

(11) Any other relevant information.

For extension applications, the criteria are virtually the same. At Paragraph 245DB(i) and 245DD(k), under (1) above, applicants need to have actually established, taken over or become a director of one or more genuine businesses and operated these business(es) genuinely while having the leave as Tier 1 Entrepreneurs. Points (2)-(4) above are converted into the following:

(12) The applicant has genuinely invested the money referred to in Table 5 of Appendix A into one or more genuine businesses in the UK to be spent for the purpose of that business or businesses; and

(13) The applicant genuinely intends to continue operating one or more businesses in the UK.

The last criteria at (5) is then repeated and makes reference to the conditions paragraph relevant for grants of extension of leave.

In terms of the list of factors for extension of leave applications at either Paragraph 245DB(j) if applying for entry clearance and if in-country at Paragraph 245DD(l), this is also virtually the same from initial applications. However, factors (8)-(10) are replaced with the following:

(14) The credibility of the financial accounts of the business(es);

(15) The credibility of the applicant's business activity in the UK, including when he had leave as a Tier 1 Entrepreneur;

(16) The credibility of the job creation for which the applicant is claiming points in Table 5;

(17) If the nature of the business requires mandatory accreditation, registration and/or insurance, whether that accreditation, registration and/or insurance has been obtained.

Lastly for ILR applications, the genuineness criteria and factors are listed at Paragraph 245DF(f)-(g). They are essentially a repeat of the criteria for extension applications:

(18) The applicant has established, taken over or become a director of one or more genuine businesses in the UK, and has genuinely operated that business or businesses while he had leave as a Tier 1 Entrepreneur; and

(19) The applicant has genuinely invested the money referred to in Table 6 into one or more businesses in the UK to be spent for the purpose of that business or businesses; and

(20) The applicant genuinely intends to continue operating one or more businesses in the UK.

The list of factors at Paragraph 245DF(g) is then exactly the same as that at Paragraphs 245DB(j) and 245DD(l) for extension applications.

The Immigration Rules confirm at each state that the decision-maker reserves the right to request additional information and evidence to support their assessment of the applicant's genuineness and to refuse the application if the information or evidence is not provided. Applicants must also be given 28 calendar days from the date of the request in order to respond.

If the assessment as to the application's credibility is negative, again the Immigration Rules at each stage confirm that no points in relation to a points-scoring requirement should be awarded. Importantly however, the decision-maker may also decide not to carry out the genuineness assessment if the application already falls for refusal on other grounds, and they would then reserve the right to carry out this assessment in any reconsideration of the decision.

In this respect, the guidance, which we will consider in more detail in the next section of this chapter, does set out for case-workers that:

> *"If you expect to refuse the application on other grounds, you can still carry out the genuine entrepreneur test, if it is likely to make the refusal decision more robust. If you do not apply the test, it can be done with any subsequent application or appeal where the Tribunal has sent the case back to the Home Office to reconsider the decision."*[3]

## USING THE HOME OFFICE GUIDANCE IN THE PREPARATION STAGES OF AN APPLICATION

The Home Office guidance *"Tier 1 (Entrepreneur) version 21"* is the most useful of the two and contains approximately 16 pages covering each application stage, which is worth consulting. In the following paragraphs, I have tried to extract the most salient parts, which applicants and practitioners may wish to bear in mind.

The guidance makes clear that case-workers will try and assess an applicant's genuineness as a paper exercise first if they hold doubts over the credibility of an application. If the case-worker then needs further information in order to complete this paper assessment, the guidance states that they must allow the applicant 28 calendar days from the date of the request to submit further

3 Tier 1 (Entrepreneur) Version 21.0 published on 16th January 2018 p.26

evidence. Note the lack of discretion in setting the time-limit for the provision of further evidence, which is also contained in the Rules themselves.

In the event that case-workers determine that it will not be possible to assess the credibility of an application on the papers, they may invite the applicant to interview either in person, by telephone or video-conferencing. In contrast, note the discretionary aspect of whether to invite an applicant to an interview. The guidance then focuses on each stage of the procedure summarised above.

Paper assessments

Pages 29-32 of the guidance set out the paper consideration and its mechanisms for requesting further documents with a useful table setting out the relevant time-scales at pp.31-32. The guidance stresses that case-workers can refuse an application without requesting any further information, evidence or inviting them for an interview if the applicant falls for refusal because they do not meet the points requirement for entry clearance to be granted and/or because general ground(s) for refusal apply.

Notably, if the case-worker intends to conduct a paper only assessment, they must (note mandatory again) consult a manager to make sure that the proposed course of action is fair and proportionate. Applicants and practitioners will not ordinarily know whether this course of action was followed but it may be worth requesting a copy of the applicant's file under the Data Protection Act 1998, through what is known as the Subject Access Bureau at the Home Office, as this should disclose the case-worker's notes and decision-making process. If such a procedure was not and arguably should have been followed, there may there lie a fairly straight forward challenge on procedural grounds. You should be aware however that such a challenge may not ultimately be sufficient to defeat a refusal so ideally, a challenge on substantial grounds should also accompany any procedural attack.

Similarly, case-workers are instructed at p. 29 that they must complete a genuine entrepreneur test form when assessing the credibility of the migrant and/or their funds. This is a document that is not necessarily disclosed to the applicant as a matter of course. So, it is worth trying to obtain a copy by either requesting its specific disclosure or through a Subject Access Bureau request.

<u>Interview stage</u>

Page 33 sets out the procedure for the case-worker to follow when seeking to arrange an interview. Page 34 onwards focuses on the procedure for the actual interview and is therefore more useful for applicants and practitioners to familiarise themselves with.

Firstly, case-workers are reminded that they must book an interpreter is one is wanted or needed by an applicant. This is always a bit of a bug-bear with applicants as they are often, and understandably, keen to demonstrate their English language ability. However, it cannot be reiterated enough in my view that interviews can be stressful environments, interviewers can have accents which are difficult to understand particularly for foreign nationals and business terminology is not the easiest. An interpreter may therefore provide an applicant with some comfort and may in the end help to ensure a smoother interviewing process.

At page 35, the guidance contains a list of further documents, which the case-worker may request in order to assist them in their assessment. The list is not exhaustive but acts a general guide. I have used this list most often to advise clients as to what documents they may think of including in their application in order to pre-empt any concern or certainly to have available in case any such request materialises or for some other reason, there is a need to submit these further down the line. The list includes the following:

- *a curriculum vitae (CV) to assess the applicant's previous experience in the field and in business*
- *a business plan and any market research to assess how much consideration the applicant has put into starting their business: this information can be purchased as a package, so plans that appear general may provide an indication of how genuine the applicant is*
- *evidence of appropriate accreditation, registration or insurance for the relevant business section (if the business is established)*
- *financial information overseen by a bank - for example, a small business loan*
- *hierarchy charts of larger businesses*
- *evidence of advertising*
- *contracts showing trading, if the business is established*

- *tax documentation (for example, returns or evidence of registration with HMRC) but only if the business is actually trading: non-trading businesses may still be registered*
- *affidavit from any mentors: for example, if the applicant is being mentored by a member of the British Business Angels Association*
- *evidence of previous businesses owned by the applicant*
- *details of trading premises, and permissions if the business is trading in the applicant's home*
- *evidence of investment*
- *evidence of job creation*

There is also a reminder that for entrepreneurial teams, information on the formation of the team could aid the case-worker's assessment, such as information on how they met and why they decided to form a team. In my view, this should be provided in any event with the initial application by way of a narrative either in the form of an applicant/client statement or in a covering letter, but it may be that further information arises out of this so teams should be prepared accordingly if requested to attend an interview.

Interview records

Caseworkers are also instructed at page 35 on 'record keeping'. Due to the importance of this and the fact that this is rarely followed, the short paragraph is worth re-producing *verbatim* with emphasis added:

> *"Record keeping*
>
> *Interviewing is a business as usual practice. Interview records must be concurrent and you must record all interviews exactly. You must give a copy of the interview notes to the applicant or their representatives, if they ask for one."*

As we can see, the obligation only arises if an applicant or their representative requests for a copy of the interview notes. In my experience, it is not common for representatives to accompany applicants to these types of interview. However, applicants should remember and be advised to request a copy of the notes at the conclusion of the interview. Most often however, nerves and relief get in the way at the end of the interview! If applicants are represented, it may be good practice to send applicants to their interview with a short letter drafted by their representative confirming their authority to act on the applicant's behalf and requesting a copy of the interview notes to be handed over to the applicant at the conclusion of the interview.

Again, I cannot stress the need for this enough as it seems near on impossible to obtain the interview notes after the event. The questions and answers relied upon by the Home Office will invariably be cited in the refusal and seemingly, in the Home Office's view, this is often seen as being sufficient by way of disclosure! This obviously does not provide the recipient with the full picture as there may be other questions on the same topic, which were answered perfectly reasonably further down in the interview and which, funnily enough, are not relied upon and cited by the Home office in the refusal.

Repeated requests for a copy of the interview notes post-interview do seemingly go ignored as do requests in any pre-action protocol letter sent in advance of any judicial review claim. This makes advising a client on the merits of any potential challenge and ultimately preparing a judicial review statement of grounds fairly tricky, which is why obtaining the notes straight after the interview is a must. This is also despite a very clear instruction at page 38 of the guidance for there to be a detailed refusal letter and for the transcript of the interview (if available) to support any decision as refusals on the grounds of genuineness are *"subjective"*.

In the alternative of having the full official record of the interview notes, I would advise applicants to jot down as much of the interview questions and answers that they can remember as contemporaneously to the interview as they can. This 'home-made' record should not be disclosed but can nonetheless be useful to give a flavour of the interview and whether there is a different perspective to be had from that taken in the Home Office refusal.

Converting the interview into a decision

Pages 37-8 set out what happens on the Home Office side of things after the interview, such as the steps to take if an applicant fails to attend the actual interview. These pages also confirm that interestingly, it is the 'genuine entrepreneur team' who will assess the application even if the interviewer notes that, in the interviewer's opinion, the applicant appears credible or not credible as an entrepreneur applicant. This means that, in the case of a favourable assessment by the interviewer, the genuine entrepreneur team may form a different view and a refusal can still ensue. This is why disclosure is important as getting hold of the interviewer's notes could be very useful in an onward challenge since these would not only support the applicant's case but they are also a record from the person, who is arguably best placed at the Home Office to assess an applicant's credibility.

## PRACTICAL TIPS AND THE USE OF CASE-LAW

Interestingly, in the context of genuine or non-genuine applications, the Migration Advisory Committee's review of the Tier 1 Entrepreneur and Graduate Entrepreneur routes notes the following from the Home Office's perspective:

> 3.45 *In the more recent Home Office intelligence assessment provided to us, the Home Office stated that the most common reason for an application being referred by caseworkers for potential further investigation was a suspicion that it was put together by an unscrupulous immigration adviser. These are cases where an immigration adviser is suspected of producing an application and business plan from generic templates, without significant input from the applicant. Types of activity identified include immigration advisers registering basic websites on behalf of the proposed business, providing advertising materials and contracts, and providing business plans presenting industry and market research.*

The Committee also reviewed a sample of Home Office files and concluded that:

> 4.47 *Approximately 40 per cent of the out-of-country applicants that we sampled were refused after interview. In most cases the applicant was unable to show sufficient knowledge about their business plan, or had no evidence to show that they had carried out any market research. There were a few cases where the caseworker had commented that large parts of the business plan seemed to have been taken from generic examples from a commercial website providing off-the-shelf business plans.*

This assessment does also tally with my own experience of Home Office refusals on genuineness grounds. One of the most common features in refusal decisions in initial leave applications is the Home Office concern that an applicant has not carried any or sufficient market research when formulating their business plan and proposal and that the applicant has been unable to show how they would be competitive and acquire a reasonable share of the market.

It is also clear that the Home Office will conduct checks over the internet to verify the contents of the business plan and whether large parts are lifted from templates or recycled from application to application. To a certain extent, there is nothing wrong from using templates and lawyers will know that templates can often be an essential drafting tool! What is important however is for applicants to ensure that any sections of their business plan, or for that matter any other document that is produced for the purposes of their application, and which are specific to their case and business proposal, are sufficiently tailored. It is also essential for applicants to have an excellent knowledge of their business plan and other business generated documents even if they have commissioned substantial assistance from business or management consultants in drafting these. A lack of knowledge will most often be perceived by the Home office as an indication of a lack of credibility on the part of the applicant.

As they say, "knowledge is power", and I have found that this can be at the source of many problems encountered by applicants when applying for initial leave or extension applications. As we have seen from the section above on the use of Home Office guidance and interviews, a refusal on the grounds of genuineness will often be grounded on an interview with the applicant and their team member if the application is from an entrepreneurial team.

Interviews of entrepreneur teams can often be the most problematic as each team member would usually be subjected to a separate interview. During these interviews, the range of questions will often vary but each applicant is usually asked the same sort of questions including questions about each other. If responses do not tally, the Home Office will usually hold this against the applicants.

When considering such interview records (if you have them), it is important to assess the questions asked of each applicant as it is often the case that the interviewer is not particularly careful or diligent and they may not phrase what is perhaps designed to be the same question in the same way when asking each applicant. It is therefore reasonable to point out that a differently phrased question may attract a different response. However, team members should be prepared and should know each other's roles inside out in the event that these are different.

Lastly, by way of a general tip, it is important for applicants to have the confidence to say if they are confused or if they are nervous as we know that this is often a source of mistakes being made during an interview. If an applicant does not express this, it is difficult to rely on such difficulties further down the line in a challenge. It is also advisable for applicants to be clear when they can or cannot answer a question and if they cannot, to try and show where the information can be found. For example, if an applicant is asked how much was spent by their business on advertising and marketing in the last year, if this figure is not to hand, it should be possible for the applicant to give a rough one and to then sign-post the interviewer to where this can be checked in, for example, the business' financial accounts.

When seeking to challenge a decision grounded on genuineness points, there are two pieces of case-law in particular that are useful to consider and cite in support of any submissions made. These are *R (on the application of Mushtaq) v Entry Clearance Officer of Islamabad, Pakistan (ECO – procedural fairness) IJR* [2015] UKUT 224 (IAC) and *R (on the application of Anjum) v Entry Clearance Officer, Islamabad (entrepreneur – business expansion – fairness generally)* [2017] UKUT 00406 (IAC). Both determinations are from the then-President of the Upper Tribunal, Mr Justice McCloskey, and both are essential in my view when trying to plead the common law principle of fairness and when trying to attack the decision-making process attached to a Home Office interview.

Taking *Mushtaq* first, this is actually a case concerning a Tier 4 student entry clearance but since it considers in detail Home Office or entry clearance officer interviewing techniques and interpretation, there is no difficulty in applying this case-law to a different context. Concerning the principle of fairness, McCloskey J summarises how this principle has been applied within this jurisdiction. He also summarises the fifth and sixth general principles enunciated in *R v Secretary of State for the Home Department, ex parte Doody* [1993] 1 All ER 151, [1994] 1 AC 531 and how these have particular significance to the case being considered in *Mushtaq*. The summary at Paragraph 9 does act as a short review of this jurisprudence and as an aide-memoir to the other judgments, which may be worth consulting when preparing submissions on these points.

Before considering *Mustaq* further, it is however worth re-producing all six principles established by Lord Mustill in *ex parte Doody*:

> *"What does fairness require in the present case? My Lords, I think it unnecessary to refer by name or to quote from, any of the other cited authorities in which the court have explained what is essentially an intuitive judgement. They are far too well known. From them, I derive that (1) where an Act of Parliament confers an administrative power there is a presumption that it will be exercised in a manner which is fair in all the circumstances. (2) The standards of fairness are not immutable. They may change with the passage of time, both in the general and in their application to decisions of a particular type. (3) The principles of fairness are not to be applied by rote identically in every situation. What fairness demands is dependent on the context of the decision and this is to be taken into account in all its aspects. (4) An essential feature of the context is the statute which creates the discretion, as regards both its language and the shape of the legal administrative system within which the decision is taken. (5) Fairness will very often require that a person who may be adversely affected by the*

> *decision will have an opportunity to make representations on his own behalf either before the decision is taken with a view to producing a favourable result; or after it is taken, with a view to procuring its modification; or both. (6) Since the person affected cannot usually make worthwhile representations without knowing what factors may weigh against his interests fairness will very often require that he is informed of the gist of the case which he has to answer."*

Otherwise, following a very detailed analysis of the questions and answers of the Home Office interview in *Mushtaq*, the judicial head-note extracted the following guidance:

> *(i) The common law principles of procedural fairness apply to the decision making processes of Entry Clearance Officers ("ECOs").*
>
> *(ii) ECO interviews serve the basic twofold purpose of enabling applications to be probed and investigated and, simultaneously, giving the applicant a fair opportunity to respond to potentially adverse matters. The ensuing decision must accord with the principles of procedural fairness.*
>
> *(iii) A breach of the "Case Worker Guidance" may render the decision of an ECO unlawful. As a general rule, a challenge advanced on this basis will succeed only where Wednesbury irrationality or a material procedural irregularity is established.*

The second paragraph is normally the most useful to rely on and to cite extensively. This guidance also confirms (together with the fifth and sixth principles in *Doody*) that an applicant should be given a fair opportunity to respond to potentially adverse matters. In my experience, when it comes to Tier 1 Entrepreneur interviews, it is rarely the case that a Home Office or entry clearance officer interviewer puts to an applicant that they are concerned with their credibility or that a particular aspect of their application or interview answer gives them a cause for concern when it comes to the applicant's genuineness. This is arguably unfair.

The way interviews are conducted and generally used in a genuineness assessment can also be used in an onward challenge. As we considered earlier in this chapter, it is usually the case that the person interviewing the applicant(s) is not the same person who undertakes the ultimate genuineness assessment and decision in the application. This means that very often, questions which are said to have generated a vague or unsatisfactory response in the refusal letter were not followed up or probed by the interviewer.

Similarly, if one or some of the interview answers by an applicant are used against them in the refusal for amounting to an inconsistency, either internally within the interview or compared to some other documents or aspect of the application, very often this concern or inconsistency has not been pointed out to the applicant in the interview for their response or comment. There may very well be a reasonable or innocent explanation to such a concern, which could have been clarified at the interview had the applicant been given such an opportunity.

For these reasons therefore, the same type of forensic analysis of the interview, which was conducted in the determination of *Mushtaq,* should be carried forward in all interviews where genuineness has been an issue. This very may enable a challenge on the grounds of fairness and possibly also on the grounds of irrationality and failure to consider relevant matters.

The other part of *Mushtaq*, which in my view is also worth citing is Paragraph 19:

> *"I make one concluding observation. The choice of questions and words in ECO interviews requires care and planning. Ambiguous words and phrases are to be avoided. Furthermore, fairness will often require that the interviewer invite the subject to clarify or expand an answer or probe a response. These simple mechanisms will also illuminate the court's assessment of whether any ensuing adverse decision was preordained. The nationals of impoverished and deprived countries who have invested large sums of money and whose admission to the United Kingdom is lawful if they satisfy the requirements of the relevant legal rules are deserving of no less."*

Note the reference to 'preordained decisions', which to many practitioners am sure is a frequent impression. The last sentence is also refreshing for applicants and applicant representatives.

The second piece of case-law is more recent: *R (on the application of Anjum) v Entry Clearance Officer, Islamabad (entrepreneur – business expansion – fairness generally)* [2017] UKUT 00406 (IAC). You may recall this case in the context of what amounts to 'investments' and whether the purchase of a second business in order to expand the applicant's own business meets the requirements of Paragraph 245D of the Immigration Rules. The case of *Anjum* also looked at the fairness of interviews, with the second paragraph of the judicial head-note summarising the guidance as follows:

> *"(ii) An immigration interview may be unfair, thereby rendering the resulting decision unlawful, where inflexible structural adherence to prepared questions excludes the spontaneity necessary to repeat or clarify obscure questions and/or to probe or elucidate answers given."*

McCloskey J cites here too the famous passage from Lord Musthill's judgment in *ex parte Doody* at Paragraph 20 when he cites from another decision of the Upper Tribunal which had recently considered the doctrine of procedural fairness: *R (AM) v Secretary of State for the Home Department* [2017] UKUT 262 (IAC). The opening comments at Paragraph 76 of this determination cited at Paragraph 20 of *Anjum* are also worth citing in order to stress the general application of these principles and their association with the EU and ECHR legal rules:

> *"While the decision of the House of Lords in R v SSHD, ex parte Doody and Others [1994] 1 AC 531 involved a very different context, namely the release of prisoners sentenced to life imprisonment, I consider that the terms in which Lord Mustill devised his celebrated code of procedural fairness makes clear that it is of general application. Furthermore, its association with the EU and ECHR legal rules and principles outlined above is unmistakable. The passage in question (at page 560D) is not susceptible to cherry picking and demands reproduction in full: (…)" (and you have the full passage above).*

Further into Paragraph 20 and 21 of the *Anjum* determination, McCloskey J considers two other authorities, which analysed interviews of immigrants and in particular, problems of interpretation, difficulties in the transcribing of interview records, the Court's encouragement of tape recording interviews and so on. The two authorities are *R (Mapah) v Secretary of State for the Home Department* [2003] All ER (D) 338 (Feb), (2003) Times, 5 March, [2003] EWHC 306 (Admin) and *R (Dirshe) v Secretary of State for the Home Department* [2005] 1 WLR 2685, [2005] EWCA Civ 421. Albeit these cases focus on asylum interviews, as can be seen from the Upper Tribunal's emphasis in *Anjum*, the guidance has wider application as well. The Court of Appeal in *Dirshe* also noted at Paragraph 14, as is extracted at Paragraph 21 of *Anjum*, that:

> *"The record of the interview is created by the interviewing officer, who is acting on behalf of the respondent. It follows that fairness requires that the procedure should give to the applicant an adequate opportunity to challenge its reliability or adequacy."*

For some considerable time now, there is an in-built procedure and period of time for asylum applicants to make representations following their interview and once they have been provided with a record of this. With the rationale that applicants can correct any mistakes or clarify any aspect of their interview. There is no such procedure in Tier 1 Entrepreneur cases when interviews are requested and as we have seen in the previous section of this chapter, applicants are rarely provided with a copy of their interview record.

In *Anjum*, the Upper Tribunal concluded that *"(t)he single enduring reason for the refusal of the Applicant's Tier 1 application was based on a series of interview answers which on any reasonable and fair showing demanded further probing and clarification"*. As mentioned above, if applicants and practitioners can consider the full contents of an interview and show the causal links between the interview contents and the refusal as well as the deficiencies in the interview process, this should assist in building the blocs for a challenge against the refusal on grounds of unfairness and possibly irrationality as well.

# CHAPTER FIVE
# HOW TO CHALLENGE A REFUSAL TO GRANT A TIER 1 (ENTREPRENEUR) APPLICATION

In this chapter, we will see that since the coming into force of the various appeal provisions of the Immigration Act 2014, challenging a refusal in a Tier 1 Entrepreneur application has become a lot more difficult. We will first have a brief look at these statutory provisions, which changed the face of the immigration appeal regime and which created the new system of administrative reviews. We will then take a closer look at the potential strategies and heads of challenge applicants may wish to consider when seeking to challenge a refusal in a Tier Entrepreneur application.

## THE MECHANICS OF A CHALLENGE POST-IMMIGRATION ACT 2014

Ever since the PBS came into being, there have not been any statutory appeals against refusals of entry clearance applications. The only remedy in these instances became that of an administrative review application and potentially a judicial review claim after that or failing that, a fresh application.

This then encroached into in-country applications with the coming into force of the Immigration Act 2014. The commencement orders bringing the abolition of in-country statutory appeals by way of a phased approach are very dense pieces of drafting so I will not go into these in detail. When it comes to Tier 1 Entrepreneurs, what applicants and practitioners need to know is that applications made on or after 2nd March 2015 will no longer attract a statutory appeal to the immigration tribunals and will be subject to the administrative review application system. The time-limit to lodge an application for an administrative review is usually 14 days from the date of being served with the refusal decision.

If a Tier 1 Entrepreneur application is made before 2nd March 2015 and is made "in-time", i.e. before the expiry of any leave to enter or remain, there are transitional arrangements in place so as to preserve the statutory right of appeal.

In both instances of entry clearance and post-2nd March 2015 applications, those seeking to qualify under the Tier 1 Entrepreneur route will not be able to challenge a negative administrative review decision, save by way of a judicial review claim. For further guidance on the administrative review process, applicants and practitioners should consult Appendix AR of the Immigration Rules. This lists *inter alia* the definition of an 'eligible decision', i.e. what can be challenged by way of administrative review, the possible outcomes of such a review, what will be considered as part of the review and what amounts to a case-working error. The accompanying Home Office guidance *"Administrative Review – version 8.0"* published on 6th April 2017 is also useful to consult.

On the whole, it is very difficult to succeed in an application for administrative review and many practitioners and applicants feel that it is almost a case of going through the motions so that they can then consider challenging the decision by way of a judicial review or by submitting a fresh application. It is also confirmed in Home Office guidance that the time-limit for a claim for judicial review claim would only start to run from the date of service of the administrative review decision, which maintained the initial refusal[1]. Although I always tend to count the time running from the date of the administrative review decision rather than the date of service.

One of the worst features of the administrative review system is that the Home Office will only consider fresh evidence, i.e. which was not initially submitted in support of the application or following a request of the Home Office during the application process, in very limited circumstances. These exceptions mainly relate to cases where the Home Office alleges that the applicant submitted a false document or made false representations. In those cases, applicants have the right to submit new evidence for the sole purpose of trying to defeat the allegations made against them. Another category of exception is if the case-worker failed to apply the 'evidential flexibility' provisions of the Immigration Rules, which will be considered in more detail in the next section of this chapter below.

However, this bar on new evidence in all other cases is particularly problematic when the Home Office issues a refusal on the grounds of genuineness. Very often, the Home Office does not request applicants for further documents or information, which could go towards alleviating the Home Office's concerns and the very first time that an applicant hears of the concerns, which led to their application being refused, is in the refusal decision itself. When this is coupled with an inability to remedy such a concern by way of an administrative review, the system does seem rather farcical and unfair.

---

1 p.71 of "Administrative Review" Home Office guidance

Applicants are then faced with a choice of either submitting a fresh application as soon as possible or lodging an application for administrative review only for this to fail and to open the way for a potential judicial review claim. However, this is costly and the level of uncertainty can be too much for many applicants. This also rather flies in the face of McCloskey's observations at Paragraph 19 of *Mushtaq*, which we considered in the last chapter in the context of the genuineness test – that *"the nationals of impoverished and deprived countries who have invested large sums of money and whose admission to the United Kingdom is lawful if they satisfy the requirements of the relevant legal rules are deserving of no less."* I would seek to add though that the nationals of other wealthy countries are also deserving of no less!

## THE USE OF THE 'EVIDENTIAL FLEXIBILITY' POLICY AND IMMIGRATION RULES AND OTHER HEADS OF CHALLENGE

As mentioned briefly above, one of the instances where the Home Office will accept that it should consider new evidence in the context of an administrative review application is if an applicant can successfully show that the Home Office should have applied the 'evidential flexibility' provisions of the Immigration Rules before refusing the application.

The provisions are set out at Paragraph 245AA of the Immigration Rules and catch all categories of applications under the PBS:

## *245AA. Documents not submitted with applications*

*(a) Subject to sub-paragraph (b) and where otherwise indicated, where Part 6A or any appendices referred to in Part 6A state that specified documents must be provided, the decision maker (that is the Entry Clearance Officer, Immigration Officer or the Secretary of State) will only consider documents received by the Home Office before the date on which the application is considered.*

*(b) If the applicant has submitted the specified documents and:*

*(i) some of the documents within a sequence have been omitted (for example, if one page from a bank statement is missing) and the documents marking the beginning and end of that sequence have been provided; or*

*(ii) a document is in the wrong format (for example, if a letter is not on letterhead paper as specified); or*

*(iii) a document is a copy and not an original document; or*

*(iv) a document does not contain all of the specified information;*

*the decision maker may contact the applicant or his representative in writing, and request the correct documents. Such a request will only be made once, and the requested documents must be received at the address specified in the request within 10 working days of the date of the request.*

*(c) Documents will not be requested under sub-paragraph (b) where:*

*(i) a specified document has not been submitted (for example an English language certificate is missing); or*

*(ii) where the decision maker does not think that submission of the missing or correct documents will lead to a grant because the application will be refused for other reasons.*

*(d) If the applicant has submitted a specified document:*

*(i) in the wrong format; or*

*(ii) which is a copy and not an original document; or*

*(iii) which does not contain all of the specified information, but the missing information is verifiable from:*

*(1) other documents submitted with the application; or*

*(2) the website of the organisation which issued the document; or*

*(3) the website of the appropriate regulatory body;*

*the decision maker may request the correct document under sub-paragraph (b), or may grant the application despite the error or omission, if satisfied that the specified documents are genuine and the applicant meets all the other requirements of the Rules.*

The provisions that are most commonly used are (b) and (d). The Home Office practice and how it utilises these provisions is extremely varied in my experience. Paragraph 245AA is also accompanied with Home Office guidance, which is there to aid interpretation of the Immigration Rules: *"Evidential flexibility: points-based system – Version 8.0"* published on 24th November 2016.

This guidance is also referred to at pp.25-26 of the Tier 1 Entrepreneur guidance, which we looked at in detail in the fourth 'genuineness' chapter. Caseworkers are instructed here to decide whether to apply the evidential flexibility rules and/or verify any of the documents supplied by the applicant and that if they decide to apply evidential flexibility, they must follow the published guidance on this.

The main pieces of case-law, which can be useful to consult when considering whether to mount a challenge under the heading of 'evidential flexibility', are *Mandalia v Secretary of State for the Home Department* [2016] 4 All ER 189, [2015] UKSC 59 and *SH (Pakistan) v Secretary of State for the Home Department* [2016] All ER (D) 277 (Feb), [2016] EWCA Civ 426. However, you should be aware that both these authorities were considering the 'evidential flexibility' policy, which was then in force prior to and for some time, in parallel of the Immigration Rules at Paragraph 245AA so not all of the guidance contained therein would be relevant to applications at present. Indeed, the latest case-law in this jurisprudence, that of *Mudiyanselage v Secretary of State for the Home Department* [2018] 4 WLR 5, [2018] EWCA Civ 65, concluded that the sole authority for the exercise of a case-worker's discretion under the 'evidential flexibility' provisions is now within the Immigration Rules.

Underhill LJ also added the following cautionary note in *Mudiyanselage* at Paragraph 56:

> *"The clear message of those authorities, including Mandalia, is that occasional harsh outcomes are a price that has to be paid for the perceived advantages of the PBS process. It is important not to lose sight of the fact that the responsibility is on applicants to ensure that the letter of the requirements of the PBS is observed: though that may sometimes require a good deal of care and attention to detail, because of the regrettable complexity of the Rules, it will normally be possible to get it right."*

Otherwise, the other heads of challenge, that applicants and practitioners are left with when seeking to challenge a refusal is to argue that the Home Office did not apply the Immigration Rules correctly, which is a ground for review included in Appendix AR for administrative reviews.

As mentioned above, in the absence of statutory appeals, a judicial review claim is the only remedy left in the event that the administrative review application has failed if an applicant does not wish to submit a fresh application instead or if there are good merits to show that the Home Office decision is unlawful.

In the forum of a judicial review, there are limitations since the Tribunal's powers are arguably only supervisory. Generally speaking, in public law, there are three categories of judicial review grounds, which are commonly pleaded: illegality, procedural unfairness and irrationality. Illegality would be quite a rare challenge to mount in immigration judicial reviews but there may still be instances where this head may be relevant. I would also include as sub-heading perhaps a 'failure to consider relevant matters' or 'weight being attached to immaterial matters'.

We have looked at examples of unfairness being used as a head of challenge in the fourth chapter of this guide in the context of 'genuineness' assessments. Examples of a decision or conclusion being irrational may be if the Home Office judged an applicant not genuine on the basis of an interview without attaching any weight or arguably even considering the applicant's business history if they are, for example, very successful in their own business in their own country already.

# MORE BOOKS BY LAW BRIEF PUBLISHING

A selection of our other titles available now:-

| |
|---|
| 'A Practical Guide to Solicitor and Client Costs' by Robin Dunne |
| 'Artificial Intelligence – The Practical Legal Issues' by John Buyers |
| 'A Practical Guide to Wrongful Conception, Wrongful Birth and Wrongful Life Claims' by Rebecca Greenstreet |
| 'Occupiers, Highways and Defective Premises Claims: A Practical Guide Post-Jackson – 2nd Edition' by Andrew Mckie |
| 'A Practical Guide to Financial Ombudsman Service Claims' by Adam Temple & Robert Scrivenor |
| 'A Practical Guide to the Law of Enfranchisement and Lease Extension' by Paul Sams |
| 'A Practical Guide to Marketing for Lawyers – 2nd Edition' by Catherine Bailey & Jennet Ingram |
| 'A Practical Guide to Advising Schools on Employment Law' by Jonathan Holden |
| 'Certificates of Lawful Use and Development: A Guide to Making and Determining Applications' by Bob Mc Geady & Meyric Lewis |
| 'A Practical Guide to the Law of Dilapidations' by Mark Shelton |
| 'A Practical Guide to the 2018 Jackson Personal Injury and Costs Reforms' by Andrew Mckie |
| 'A Guide to Consent in Clinical Negligence Post-Montgomery' by Lauren Sutherland QC |
| 'A Practical Guide to Running Housing Disrepair and Cavity Wall Claims: 2nd Edition' by Andrew Mckie & Ian Skeate |
| 'A Practical Guide to the General Data Protection Regulation (GDPR)' by Keith Markham |
| 'A Practical Guide to Digital and Social Media Law for Lawyers' by Sherree Westell |
| 'A Practical Guide to Holiday Sickness Claims – 2nd Edition' by Andrew Mckie & Ian Skeate |

| |
|---|
| 'A Practical Guide to Inheritance Act Claims by Adult Children Post-Ilott v Blue Cross' by Sheila Hamilton Macdonald |
| 'A Practical Guide to Elderly Law' by Justin Patten |
| 'Arguments and Tactics for Personal Injury and Clinical Negligence Claims' by Dorian Williams |
| 'A Practical Guide to QOCS and Fundamental Dishonesty' by James Bentley |
| 'A Practical Guide to Drone Law' by Rufus Ballaster, Andrew Firman, Eleanor Clot |
| 'Practical Mediation: A Guide for Mediators, Advocates, Advisers, Lawyers, and Students in Civil, Commercial, Business, Property, Workplace, and Employment Cases' by Jonathan Dingle with John Sephton |
| 'Practical Horse Law: A Guide for Owners and Riders' by Brenda Gilligan |
| 'A Comparative Guide to Standard Form Construction and Engineering Contracts' by Jon Close |
| 'A Practical Guide to Compliance for Personal Injury Firms Working With Claims Management Companies' by Paul Bennett |
| 'A Practical Guide to the Landlord and Tenant Act 1954: Commercial Tenancies' by Richard Hayes & David Sawtell |
| 'A Practical Guide to Personal Injury Claims Involving Animals' by Jonathan Hand |
| 'A Practical Guide to Psychiatric Claims in Personal Injury' by Liam Ryan |
| 'Introduction to the Law of Community Care in England and Wales' by Alan Robinson |
| 'A Practical Guide to Dog Law for Owners and Others' by Andrea Pitt |
| 'Ellis and Kevan on Credit Hire – 5th Edition' by Aidan Ellis & Tim Kevan |
| 'RTA Allegations of Fraud in a Post-Jackson Era: The Handbook – 2nd Edition' by Andrew Mckie |
| 'RTA Personal Injury Claims: A Practical Guide Post-Jackson' by Andrew Mckie |
| 'On Experts: CPR35 for Lawyers and Experts' by David Boyle |
| 'An Introduction to Personal Injury Law' by David Boyle |
| 'A Practical Guide to Claims Arising From Accidents Abroad and Travel Claims' by Andrew Mckie & Ian Skeate |
| 'A Practical Guide to Cosmetic Surgery Claims' by Dr Victoria Handley |

| |
|---|
| 'A Practical Guide to Chronic Pain Claims' by Pankaj Madan |
| 'A Practical Guide to Claims Arising from Fatal Accidents' by James Patience |
| 'A Practical Approach to Clinical Negligence Post-Jackson' by Geoffrey Simpson-Scott |
| 'A Practical Guide to Personal Injury Trusts' by Alan Robinson |
| 'Employers' Liability Claims: A Practical Guide Post-Jackson' by Andrew Mckie |
| 'A Practical Guide to Subtle Brain Injury Claims' by Pankaj Madan |
| 'The Law of Driverless Cars: An Introduction' by Alex Glassbrook |
| 'A Practical Guide to Costs in Personal Injury Cases' by Matthew Hoe |
| 'A Practical Guide to Alternative Dispute Resolution in Personal Injury Claims – Getting the Most Out of ADR Post-Jackson' by Peter Causton, Nichola Evans, James Arrowsmith |
| 'A Practical Guide to Personal Injuries in Sport' by Adam Walker & Patricia Leonard |
| 'The No Nonsense Solicitors' Practice: A Guide To Running Your Firm' by Bettina Brueggemann |
| 'Baby Steps: A Guide to Maternity Leave and Maternity Pay' by Leah Waller |
| 'The Queen's Counsel Lawyer's Omnibus: 20 Years of Cartoons from The Times 1993-2013' by Alex Steuart Williams |

These books and more are available to order online direct from the publisher at www.lawbriefpublishing.com, where you can also read free sample chapters. For any queries, contact us on 0844 587 2383 or mail@lawbriefpublishing.com.

Our books are also usually in stock at www.amazon.co.uk with free next day delivery for Prime members, and at good legal bookshops such as Hammicks and Wildy & Sons.

We are regularly launching new books in our series of practical day-to-day practitioners' guides. Visit our website and join our free newsletter to be kept informed and to receive special offers, free chapters, etc.

You can also follow us on Twitter at www.twitter.com/lawbriefpub.

www.ingramcontent.com/pod-product-compliance
Lightning Source LLC
LaVergne TN
LVHW022106200926
848481LV00003B/1070